EFFECTIVE PARENTING

An  ON THE FUTURE...

EFFECTIVE PARENTING
An  ON THE FUTURE...

By

S.C. Arora

Vice-Chairman
LPS Global School
D-196/2, Sector-51, Noida
&
Formerly Vice-Chairman
Lotus Valley International School, Noida
&
Former Principal Apeejay Schools

Gullybaba Publishing House Pvt. Ltd.

GULLYBABA PUBLISHING HOUSE PVT. LTD.

ISO 9001 & ISO 14001 Certified Co.

Regd. Office: 2525/193, 1st Floor, Onkar Nagar-A, Tri Nagar, New Delhi-110035 (Near Kanhaiya Nagar Metro Station)

Branch Office: 1A/2A, 20, Hari Sadan, Ansari Road, Daryaganj, New Delhi-110002

Ph.: 9350849407, 011-27387998

E-mail: info@gullybaba.com

Websites: GullyBaba.com, GullybabaKids.com

Edition: 2019

ISBN: 978-93-88149-71-6

Copyright© 2019, Publisher

CONTENTS

I. Get Involved in the School

II. Homework

III. Pocket-Money

IV. Exams

I. United Front (please confirm whether it is united front or Unity—In chapter is written Unity)

II. Intelligent Handling

III. Enlarge the Scope of Learning

IV. Create a Learning Atmosphere

V. Share Time with Children

VI. Play Together, Stay Together

VII. Exposure

VIII. Self-Learning

IX. Sanctions and Punishment

X. Self-Esteem

XI. Role Model

FOREWORD BY TISCA CHOPRA

Being the parent of a young child poses a daily challenge. The truths one believed in the day before no longer apply today – the child evolves faster than one can keep up.

Effective Parenting sets down certain unchanging principles that will hold good when your child is 4 and 14. That truly is a relief, when one over thinks and questions every action as a parent. Mr Arora's experience as an educator has given him insight and perspective via lacs of students he has taught, including so called 'problem kids'.

He tells us there are no 'problem kids', only unable-to-solve-the-problem parents.

Effective Parenting reveals the wisdom of the author gleaned over 50 years as an educator in some of the best institutions of the country. His massive contribution to the lives of lacs of parents and their children is unparalleled. The book covers tricky areas like pocket money, homework, parent-child tiffs, exam & peer pressure. Mr Arora suggests out of the box solutions that will be a beacon for any parent reading the book. This book is a must read for parents/grandparents who want to do their very best for their progeny.

Tisca Chopra

Actor & Author

Preface

I am dedicating this book to the children of the world who are the citizens of tomorrow. It is addressed to those adults who care about children and have to deal with them either at home or at school or in any other situation. Over the years parents have discussed with me the problems of their children and sought advice for handling them. I have not been able to give them a cut and dried solution to each distinctive problem nor do I think that a road-map exists out of every tangled situation. However, in my career of over five decades in education, I have attended conferences, read papers at different seminars, learnt from experts in the field, read books, magazines, research papers, articles in the newspapers on children and the material has been churning in my mind. As a result, something new has emerged which I am presenting to parents, grandparents and all those who are interested in the proper growth of children. I do not lay any claim to originality (All my best thoughts were stolen by the ancients —R.W. Emerson) but an amalgam of ideas does appear in the book which may be of some help to those who care to read and act. I do hope that everybody finds something useful and feels better equipped to deal with children.

It is suggested that parents do not entirely pass on the responsibility to schools for the growth of their children as there is much they can do at home. It is my conviction that each child is a masterpiece in the making: what is needed is proper chiseling and polishing. The raw diamond is bound to turn into a 'Kohinoor'. I have discovered that there are no problem children: yes, they may have some problems which need to be tackled. Children do not fail: it's the grown ups who have not mentored them well.

It will be noticed that most of the suggestions given in the book are reinforcement of common sense. All of us know how to deal with a particular situation but either due to lack of time or patience or our Indulgence in children, we sometimes do not succeed. My endeavor has been just to remind ourselves that it is possible to find a solution to any problem if we apply our minds and do not lose our cool.

The examples cited in the book are actual incidents, although some names have been changed for the sake of confidentiality. I would like the parents to know that they have tremendous power in their hands to influence the learning, behavior, attitudes, aspirations, character and values of their children.

I had requested some parents to send me a write-up on the strategies they adopted in bringing up their children. They are reproduced verbatim in this book. Most of these children have been my students and I know that they are doing exceedingly well in life. It would be of help to all to read these letters for strengthening their own ways of raising children. Parents' philosophy of life may not fully tally with theirs but certain useful ideas can definitely be picked up for application.

In the pages that follow I have given the distillate of my experience in dealing with school-going children. But no final word can ever be said in this complex field where each individual child requires a different treatment. Therefore, I would welcome suggestions,comments and criticism for further improvement of the book. You are also free to pose questions not addressed in this book.

Vice-Chairman   S.C. Arora
LPS Global School   busybee_1940@yahoo.com
D-196/2, Sector-51,

Noida, (U.P.), India

ACKNOWLEDGEMENTS

It is possible for an individual to have an idea but no single person can implement the same all by himself. It requires the effort of a whole team to bring things to fruition. The labour of many people have gone in in bringing out this book. I am indebted to Mr. Manish Yadav, Chairman, LPS Global School, Noida, who encouraged me to publish the book. I express my gratitude to many teachers of LPS Global School who spared their time in going through the proof and giving their input for enriching the content. I am grateful to Mrs. Helen Kant who read through the script for the final print and has made useful suggestions which have enhanced the quality of the book.

This book would not have seen the light of the day without the herculean effort of Gullybaba Publishers, who typed and retyped many times the edited version of this volume. My thanks to them.

I am most grateful to the eight parents who responded to my request and put in writing their strategies for bringing up children. I also extend my thanks to my numerous students with whom I interacted through the years and tested my theoretical knowledge which helped in giving concrete shape to my ideas expressed in this book.

I acknowledge the contribution made by many magazines, newspapers, experts in the field, research findings, seminars workshops etc. too numerous to mention, which influenced my thinking. I also take this opportunity of thanking countless parents who, over the years, brought problems of their children and gave me a chance to reflect on them and offer advice. I am indebted to those parents as well who have been captive listeners and on whom I imposed my ideas without their knowing it.

S.C. Arora

Point of View

"The college professor says:

Such rawness in pupils is a shame
Lack of preparation in HIGH SCHOOL is to blame.

But the HIGH SCHOOL teacher says:
GOOD HEAVENS! Such crudity: The boy's a fool
The fault, of course, is the MIDDLE SCHOOL.

But the MIDDLE SCHOOL teacher says:
From such stupidity may I be spared,
THEY SEND them to me so unprepared.

But the primary teacher says:
KINDERGARTEN block heads, and they call this preparation?
Worse than none at all.
But the KINDERGARTEN teacher says:
Such lack of training never did I see,
What kind of mother must that mother be?
But MOTHER has the final word,

MOTHER says:
Poor helpless CHILD: He's not to blame,
His FATHER'S people are all the same."

TINY TEACHERS

If we looked to our children,

So simple and pure.

If we looked to our children,

We could learn so much more.

If we looked to our children,

We could rise above.

If we looked to our children,

We could learn how to love.

If we looked to our children,

We could find a way to be free.

If we looked to our children,

We could learn how to see.

If we looked to our children,

Without being so stern.

If we looked to our children,

How much we could learn.

- **Cindy Kocsis**

INTRODUCTION

> *"Each human being is uniquely different, like snowflakes the human pattern is never cast twice."* **- Alice Childress**

"Everybody wants to go to heaven but nobody wants to die". Every parent wants a designer child i.e. tops in studies, very good in sports, excellent in co-curricular activities, the best debater, outstanding actor etc, but only a few put in the efforts to achieve the same: those who do, get the Kohinoor, those who don't, their children get marginalised.

Believe in PARENTING POWER! Enjoy the blessings you have received as a Parent. Remember, good parenting causes headaches, but bad parenting causes heartaches.

Whether you are a working parent or a full-time homemaker, your life is probably very busy; so many daily chores and social obligations, that need attention, clutter your mind and you are obliged to rush from one task to another. Consequently, very little time is left to be devoted to your progeny to convert him/her into a designer child. Even when the child is being attended to, we may feel irritated, angry or sad during difficult times. Our children get lazy, they make mistakes, they break precious household articles, they indulge in silly and stupid things. At times, we lose control and even smack! The anger or the sadness which overwhelms us is not without reason. But if we, as adults, also react impulsively, nothing meaningful is accomplished.

Get ready for the hardest job: Parenting is the hardest job that you have ever done or will be doing. Get ready to learn the tricks of the trade. Be prepared for different situations.

We live in a world which is largely beyond our control; we cannot stop the violence, titillating scenes, the deceptive slogans of T.V. salesmen trying to sell their goods, nor can we clamp down on the vulgarity, obscenity on the electronic and print media. Therefore, the only solution left with us is that we provide our children with tools so that they can fend for themselves later in life.

A child is a unique creation of nature, but having given birth to a child does not entitle us to become a parent as the possession of a Guitar does not make us eligible to be called a Guitarist. We will only remain biological parents if we do not put in all-round efforts. Child development is not a mini re-play of evolution which has taken centuries to come to this stage. Although it is an age of the net and jet, there are no fast elevators which can be used for bringing up children. However, there are certainly bypasses, flyovers and certain expressways to avoid the time-wasting congestion of unnecessary problems of growth. We have to take care of our child from early stages just as a plant needs tending to; support has to be provided to a sapling to avoid skewed growth. For the proper development of the genetic endowments of the child we have to spend time and lead him onto the right path. **Nature must be supplemented with nurture.**

"Education should not only train the intellect but also bring grace into the heart of man. Imagination should be fostered and emotions refined. The inquisitive mind, the intuitive heart, the sensitive spirit and the searching conscience should also be developed. Education should be for the whole man: To Think, To Feel, To Do, To Be.
- Dr. Radhakrishnan

Early Childhood and Education (3⁺ to 9 yrs)

Learning begins to take place as soon as the child is born. The child starts exploring the physical world by seeing, touching, feeling, hearing, smelling, etc. He develops physically, mentally and emotionally. His bones are being strengthened, his blood is being made and his mind is being shaped. A lot of learning has already taken place by the time a child reaches the pre-school age. At this stage rapid mental development takes place. They begin to pick up the vocabulary to express. They are very inquisitive; they tend to have many queries, they want to

know many things. Sometimes we notice that they are not interested in the expensive toy we have bought them. They will break it, remove the parts and try to see what is inside, leaving you wondering as to what is happening in their minds. They may be happier with the sound of the spoon banging on the plate but not with the sophisticated toy school bus you so lovingly brought home. They may get more interested in the box of the doll than the doll itself. They get easily frustrated when faced with difficult situations and, therefore, need parental help.

To them ghosts, witches, monsters, fairies, angels are real beings; It happens because they cannot see the world as older children or adults do. Experiential understanding has not taken roots yet and hence for them Santa Claus does come through the chimney and leave a gift for them. The fairy does visit to take away the fallen tooth kept under the pillow and leave a present in its place.

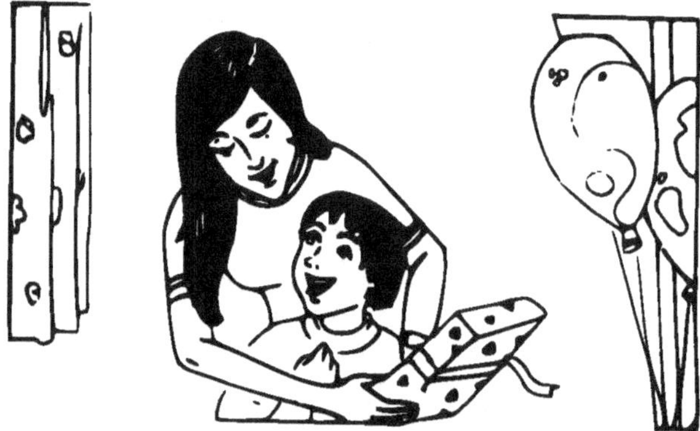

They are too young to understand the idea of abstract love and hence it has to be demonstrated through action. An ice cream, a chocolate, a kiss, a hug, a pat, a smile and playing with them are signs of love. At this age, to make them responsible you could ask them to do some small errands for you like placing the spoons in the sink, bringing a bowl for himself, bringing your sandals, putting their dirty clothes in the hamper, putting their shoes in the rack etc. As they grow older these jobs can change to making the bed, tidying their room, laying the table, etc.

On the intellectual side, parents can contribute in building up their vocabulary, thinking, imagination and communication skill. The more the parents talk to them about various things in an explanatory manner, the stronger their vocabulary would be. The child is ready to learn the names of things in the kitchen, sitting room, bedroom, bathroom, etc., He can easily learn nursery rhymes, songs, *bhajans*, hymns. Our twin students, Waiga & Dhruv Arya, memorised Panini's Ashtadhyayi (4000 sutras and shlokas) at the age of 3 ½; the ability is tremendous. The knowledge of the names of flowers, fruits, vegetables and other common things around are all within his reach. Children tend to grasp the names of colours, shapes, animals and birds by seeing their pictures or models as they progress in age.

Gradually the child can be made familiar with local surroundings like a shopping centre, a fire station, a bank etc. He can be made to interact with people doing various jobs like a tailor, a barber, a grocer, an optician, a doctor, a chemist. He can easily pick up the names and functions of electrical gadgets and equipments. Perhaps you can recall your child of $3\frac{1}{2}$ yrs able to handle the DVDs/Music systems. Imagine the confidence and enhanced self-image the child will form of himself when he is armed with this knowledge. The confidence of knowing such things will spur him to learn further with ease and pleasure. And we all know the fact that success and achievement are self-perpetuating. Therefore, children will benefit immensely if we keep affirming and celebrating even their minor successes and achievements.

The magic word in learning is CURIOSITY which should always be quenched and quickened. One doesn't have to make herculean efforts to arouse the same, as children are pre-programmed by Nature to seek the novel. "You don't have to prime the pump," aggressively. A gentle push is enough to ignite the spark.

We have to teach children how to make choices and what the consequences are for making a good or a bad choice {whether the child would like to have peas or okra (bhindi), would she like to wear red or green frock etc.}. This training will be invaluable for the rest of their lives. Throughout our lives we are making choices, friends, profession, life partner, etc.

During this age span the child is ready to **learn some values** as well. He should be able to distinguish on his own what is right and what is wrong. Various means can be adopted to inculcate such values through stories, parables, pictorial illustrations and interesting episodes from scriptures, learning and recitation of poems, group games, drawing, colouring and painting: while engaging the child in such activities, we should remember that the entire learning process has to be a source of pleasure. Obviously, it has to be done informally in a play-way method. The mind of the child is highly impressionable at this stage. We have to be extremely careful to be positive in our approach.

In our locality for the last three years every Sunday and on other holidays, I have been overhearing a grandmother telling her granddaughter (now around 7 years old) "I will break your legs if you come this side". I wonder what type of complexes and attitudes would the child grow up with.

At a young age **children have a great sense of possession**: what is theirs is theirs but what is ours is also theirs. With small children, I have often joked that if they could lend me their cap or T-shirt for a day but very rarely somebody has agreed: on the other hand whatever is lying on my table they just pick it up. Gradually as they grow older we, as adults, should start explaining to them the idea of 'sharing is caring'.

Somewhere around 6+ **their language and reasoning develop much faster:** Trot turns into gallop: they begin to observe, compare and evaluate as their thinking reaches higher order. It becomes imperative that we lead them to realise an individual's uniqueness. They should learn to tolerate and finally accept the differences among people. They should accept the different ability levels among peers and different age groups. This will instill in them the life skill of social competency which is badly needed in this world, full of diversity. He should refrain from passing caustic remarks about anybody. For this, from time to time he is to be reminded that how he would feel if others hurt his feelings. We, as parents, have a responsibility to provide opportunities for developing such character traits. One of the ways is to encourage the child to participate in group games and team work. This will satisfy the urge both for playing as well as developing friendship; these two needs are absolutely essential in this age group.

Children crave for some fun. It does not require an enormous amount of time, only a playful spirit is needed. Have fun together - Blind Man's Buff, Monopoly, Pillow Fights, Hide & Seek, Statue, Flying of paper aeroplanes and playing with frisbee, all have their benefits for children. It provides them a channel to express their feelings and emotions; let the child pretend to be a mother, father, teacher, doctor, nurse etc. Through their pretentious playing the child learns to come to terms with his environment. In addition, it spurs his imagination and the child is able to envision far away things leading to abstraction. Your daughter putting a doll to bed implies that she is ready to listen to you when you ask her to go to bed. The same applies to feeding etc. When she tells the doll "no more toffees" she is beginning to understand the harmful effect of the excessive consumption of things. As children grow older, their play and other activities become more elaborate and sophisticated. But all these pursuits remain beneficial at all ages. Our aim should not only be limited to keep encouraging but also join in whenever possible. This is bound to enhance the imagination and the self-esteem of the child.

Early years have been proven to be the most crucial years as the personality development of the child takes place in these years. If we invest in these years, the outcome will be unimaginable.

Little Eyes Upon You

There are little eyes upon you

And they're watching night and day.

There are little ears that quickly

Take in every word you say.

There are little hands all eager

To do anything you do;

And a little boy he'll be like you.

You're the little fellow's idol,

You're the wisest of the wise.

In his little mind about you

no suspicion ever rise.

He believes in you devoutly,

holds all that you say and do;

He will say and do, in your way,

when he's grown up like you.

There's a wide-eyed little fellow

who believes you're always right;

And his eyes are always opened,

and he watches day and night.

You are setting an example

every day in all you do,

For the little boy who's waiting

to grow up to be like you.

When a superior man knows the causes which make instruction successful, and those which make it of no effect, he can become a teacher of others. Thus in his teaching, he leads and does not drag: he strengthens and does not discourage: he opens the way but does not conduct to the end without the learner's own efforts. Leading and not dragging produces harmony Strengthening and not discouraging makes attainment easy. Opening the way and not conducting to the end makes the learner thoughtful. He who produces such harmony, easy attainment, and thoughtfulness may be pronounced a skillful teacher.

-Confucius, 550–478 B.C.

Heights by greatmen reached and kept,

Were not attained by sudden flight.

But they while their companions slept,

Were toiling upward in the night.

-H.W. Longfellow

Instruction increases inborn worth, and

right discipline strengthens the heart.

-Horace, 65–8 B.C

PRE-TEENS (9⁺ TO 12 YRS)

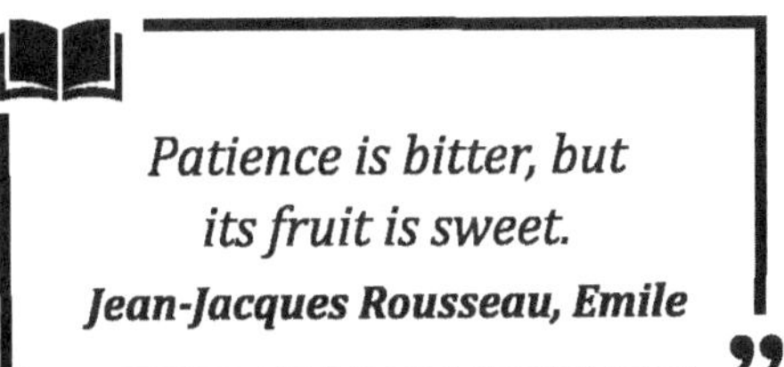

As children grow, their world begins to expand. They engage themselves in a variety of activities, be it sports, theatre, dance, music, art. **The key is to provide opportunities to participate** and in the process discover their talents and strengths. Once they have found their interest they can hone the skills. Sometimes they will need a gentle push to discover what they like. The deep interest in a particular pursuit will not necessarily lead to a career in that field but it will certainly provide the child with the attributes of discipline, concentration and diligence.

One of the most important changes that takes place in this age group is the **need for friends.** Friendship is vital for their emotional well-being. They are looking for freedom from parents yet are dependent on them. As they move away from parental control, their sense of self gets strengthened and individual identity begins to take shape. They may begin to question what adults tell them: they may not accept it, as their growth is taking place outwards. To them growing up means freedom from being told what to do all the time. In search for an identity of their own, they may unwittingly criticise or ridicule the values held by their parents. They may even question the rules made by grown-ups. Instead, they get attracted to their peers: they even begin to share their secrets with their close friends and build up quite strong bonds. They begin to get influenced by the peer group as they do not wish to be isolated. There is generally a desire to fit into the circle rather than be left out. The pre-teen's desire to be accepted as a social member often overrides his abilities to make logical, healthy decisions.

When your child makes mistakes, do not react immediately. Analyze the situations thoroughly before you react. Love your child unconditionally. No one is perfect, we have all made mistakes and will continue to.

They are intensely self-conscious and prone to self-criticism. They may begin to think of their height, weight, clothes and their appearance. Conflicts of opinions with parents are bound to arise regarding dresses, make-up, hairstyles, choice of friends etc. If the daughter wishes to wear revealing clothes, parents should explain intelligently that it may send sexual messages

which the child least expects. Make her understand that her icon whom she is trying to ape is 23 years' old and she is only 12. It is more than likely that the child will come round. However, agreeing to a little hairstyle or buying trendy shoes will not harm the child. In fact, she will shower her love for the parent for honouring her opinion.

Addition: Length of a Girl's Skirt is not a measure of her character. This is line of a letter written by Amitabh Bachchan to her granddaughters. Here is the excerpt of the letter:

"**Don't live in the shadows of people's judgement. Make your own choices in the light of your own wisdom.**

Don't let anyone make you believe that the length of your skirt is a measure of your character. Don't let anyone's opinion of who you should be friends with, dictate who you will be friends with. Don't get married for any other reason other than you want to get married.

People will talk. They shall say some terrible things. But that doesn't mean you have to listen to everyone. Never ever worry about – *log kya kahenge.* At the end of the day, you are the only one who will face the consequences of your actions, so don't let other people make your decisions for you".

They do not want to be abandoned, alone. They are still looking for affirmation and validation of their thoughts and decisions. Instead of getting irritated, we, as parents, must understand that arguments, questioning and debating on various matters by them only show that they are developing intellectually.

They find their parents as soft targets for trying out their thoughts, ideas and whims as there is the least chance of rebuttal. Even if we do not agree with their line of argument, **we should not stop listening**; it will bring its own rewards. They always need the support, encouragement, trust, confidence and guidance of parents. However, it will be a good idea to know who his/her friends are, where (s)he is spending his/her time. This will help to make course corrections.

If your son "Rahul" has just come back home after winning a match where he made 40 runs or taken two wickets or scored 2 goals etc. and if you only say "Good" and get busy with your mobile phone or the e-mail, you have not only killed the enthusiasm of the child but also alienated him. To listen to the child attentively is the key to effective communication. If "Rahul" had been appreciated, his grandparents, uncles, aunts, family-friends had been informed in his presence, his morale had been boosted and a stronger bond had been established. A pat or a hug as display of appreciation would have made him do better not only in that game but in other fields also.

Cherish his achievements: Your child comes home with good grades, show your appreciation . Your child wins a trophy in race, place the trophy alongside with your valuables.

Often I have heard complaints from parents that **their children do not listen to them. In turn, I put them a question whether they listen to them!** When your child has indulged in something wrong, you should not direct your criticism on the personality of the child but only on the event. Your getting angry or yelling will shut the child off. **The real mantra is to counsel.** Catch him doing right and praise, which will motivate him for doing further rights.

A man returned home in the evening and saw his wife (teacher) helping their child with homework.

The husband consolingly said, you have been

a great mother,

a great teacher,

a great wife.

You cannot expect to be great at all three all the time. The husband was being understanding until she replied, "OK, I won't be great wife, then..."

Control your emotions: If you express extreme emotions (anger, frustrations, etc.) in front of your child, your child is likely to copy that (children are good at imitating).

ROUGH DIAMOND

Just a diamond in the rough

is a diamond sure enough.

But before it ever sparkles

It was made of diamond stuff.

Of course, someone must find it

Or it will never be found;

Then someone must grind it

Or it will never be ground.

But when it is found, and when it is ground,

When it is burnished bright.

The diamond is everlasting

Spreading all its light.

O Teacher disappointed,

Don't say 'You've had enough'.

The worst pupil in your class

Is just a Diamond in the rough!

Let the Lessons for Reading be varied, that the youth may be made acquainted with good styles of all kinds in prose and verse, and the proper manner of reading each kind. Sometimes a well told story, a piece of a sermon, a General's speech to his soldiers, a speech in a tragedy, some part of a comedy, an ode... But let such lessons for Reading be chosen, as contain some useful instruction, whereby the Understandings or Morals of the Youth, may at the same time be improv'd.

-Benjamin Franklin, 1706-1790

Teenagers

> 
> *Children need models more than they need critics.*
>
> **- Joseph Joubert, Pensees**

Some parents start feeling dejected and rejected if the abilities and characteristics of their children are not similar to their own. They cannot think beyond their firm beliefs that if one's offspring is not the exact copy of their parents, they are bound to face difficulties in their lives. And therefore whose traits are different from the views of their parents, are considered as threat to their family.

Many parents have come and discussed with me as children enter into the age of teens; they complain that the child does not obey any more, often comes into conflicts with the family, often demands too much, spends too much time outside etc. Parents seem irritated and terribly annoyed with this type of behaviour. It appears to the parents that they are losing control over the child and hence (s)he may go astray. I can understand their fears as they are encountering this for the first time. However, they should realise that this is nothing unusual. They must not get upset at this type of attitude. Psychologists have confirmed that at this age adolescents suffer from **'Teenage Illusion'** that they know everything and are all powerful: they think perhaps their parents are 'stupid' or 'weird'. Luckily this feeling begins to taper off around 18 yrs, of age. Therefore, the assertion of independence should not be looked upon as defiance and rebellion. It will be wise to realise that the adolescent is under great stress of not only biological and physiological changes **but he/she is also looking for an identity.**

Teenage years are rife with great mental pressure because there are all round expectations—academic results, performance in other activities, behaviour, peer pressure, desire to become an adult, conflicting messages of teachers, friends, T.V., media. The reproductive organs and hormones are coming into play. The brain is switching from child to adult. They become conscious of their figure, height, weight, complexion, hairstyle etc.

I quote one instance...During my normal rounds of the school as the Head, twice I had asked Anjali Malhotra not to design her hair in a bouffant style of 2 inches as the school was not meant for fashion but for devoting time to studies and other activities. Apparently, she did not mend her ways and continued to sport the same hair-do. Once irritated as I was, I called her to my office and before admonishing I asked her the reason for not complying with the instructions. She went on to explain that **she was short-statured** and always felt embarrassed because of her height and hence the hair-do. My total perspective changed; I could understand the complex she was living with and allowed her to carry on with fluffy hair. My feelings were further confirmed that as adults we have to **understand the complexity and depth of their fears, desires and worries to be able to advise and guide.** The list of their afflictions is long. When they are unable to meet the expectations, it leads to stress.

Don't ask your children to be someone; always encourage them to be themselves. Don't tell them to be like their friend. Instead, help them to be a better person than they are now.

The teenager is actually trying to find a position for himself/ herself and that is the key task at this age. A constant anxiety is nagging his mind as to where he is headed in life. I have seen this anxiety in thousands of children who have passed through my hands. With the maturing mind the child is developing independence and wanting freedom whereas parents unknowingly wish to continue their hold on him/her still treating him as a child. (S)He wishes to know the reasons for the actions of his parents. He is redefining his social relationship. He is on his way to forming his own principles and ideals. He is looking for self-direction. He is entering adulthood: he has to reject his dependent relationship. The teenagers can think of alternative and hence there is bound to be more resistance to strict parental rules and less obedience. **But he is not rejecting the values of the parents: he is unknowingly testing them.**

These are signs of maturity and hence must be respected and honoured by parents. The parents would do well to respond to this disagreement with open discussion and always keep flexibility in mind. **Extreme dominance or permissiveness is definitely harmful.**

Read your child: In order to understand your child, you need to understand the child psychology. Try to analyze how your child feels and thinks. Respect his opinion too!

We as parents are prone to passing severe or negative judgments "You are stupid", "You are bound to fail" or we castigate our children for their untidiness, laziness or generally indisciplined ways. It doesn't work. On the contrary, there is either apathy or rebellion against the incessant nagging. We pass directives like 'you will not go to the late night party'. We pass comments like, "you are lazy" or "You are good for nothing", etc. (60 years ago my father in his innocence said to me "Tu Bahut Dhila Hai").

Don't boss around: Don't judge the child from an ivory tower, instead sit beside the child and try to understand his mind.

Instead we should try to understand the mind of the adolescent, discuss the matter and counsel by pointing out why a particular thing should not be done e.g. explain to your child that a tattoo done now cannot be erased: even if it can be, it will leave a permanent mark and it costs many thousand rupees. We should try to solve the problem e.g. when our son, Mayur, was about 14 years of age he would ask us every now and then to increase his pocket-money.

Often a conflict would arise on this issue. We sat together and discussed the matter over. Ultimately a solution emerged: an element of dearness allowance was introduced after fixing the base amount: whatever percentage of D.A. was raised by the Govt. he also became entitled to the same figure: and he always claimed the arrears too! This arrangement remained in place till he started earning for himself.

Do not meddle: Do you like people meddling in your own business? Certainly not. A child has his own world, don't create an atmosphere of meddling.

With the advent of puberty adolescents act more assertively. They are looking for company of peers where they feel more secure. Therefore, they want to go out more often. They may assert themselves by various actions viz. access to the family car and boys may want to purchase a motorcycle **more for thrill and recognition than necessity.** These are natural tendencies of teenagers and have to be understood as such. We will have to be understanding and explain to them the underlying reason. Our aim should be to listen to the adolescent attentively and counsel wherever required. Again our son Mayur (now father of two sons) then aged 17+ had come home from the sports club after losing a friendly match of Badminton. He asked the servant what he had cooked for dinner. Normal 'Dal Roti' was announced. Mayur grumbled, raised his voice, and declared that he would not eat this insipid food. Realising the situation I immediately went to the local market and brought two huge chicken sandwiches which he ate ashamedly. Next day we sat together and discussed the matter. He was asked to make the weekly menu of his choice, to avoid complaining. He made it only for a week! No such problems arose thereafter as the responsibility was passed onto him.

Every time we criticise our teenager we bring his self-esteem down by a notch or two.

Every generation faces the same fears for their children because every parent says that things are so different now than when they were teens. Teens will forever say that their parents cannot possibly understand them because times are so different, and kids are different. It really brings home the fact that no matter how much things change some things always remain the same. Teenagers are going through a tumultuous time physically, mentally and emotionally. Various researches have proved that the adolescent brain is continued to be changed as much during these years, as it did during the first three years of their lives. While your teenager may look and often act like he/she is on the brink of adulthood, they are still growing and developing, and will periodically do things that show their lack of judgment, maturity, or understanding of the laws of cause and effect. We should treat our teens with the same regard and respect that we hold for other human beings.

We are here to facilitate his growing up and not dictate to him. If our son wants to remove the silencer from the motorcycle or the daughter wants to go to a party in a short skirt or a provocative dress, it becomes imperative on our part to explain to them why it should not be done; what harm can come to them if they do so. If she is explained the danger of sexual harassment, she may come round and accept our advice but if an order is passed that 'she will not do it', it is almost certain that she, on her way to the party, may visit her friend's hostel or house, and wear the dress of her choice. After attending the party, she may reverse the process. She will start indulging in telling lies. From experience of dealing with such students, I have seen that teenagers rebel against orders *i.e.,* "You will do this" and "You will not do that". Remember! Family rules are meant to make life easy, not to strangle our children: with excessive discipline, barricades get erected between children and parents. Children will not mind conforming to discipline within the specified parameters but they would certainly resent criticism, which is immediate disapproval or fault-finding or censorious actions. Criticism is, for the most part, destructive: it is detrimental to the mental well-being of the growing child. It immediately makes him feel inferior. His/Her self-worth eroded, they lose self-confidence in their capabilities, even in their potential. **Therefore, refrain from criticising, more so in public.**

New experiences specially those with frisson of danger or the thrill of the new is a reward for the teenager: it produces feelings of intense pleasure. That is why we find cases of sneaking out at night, fast driving, using slang etc. They are looking for novelty all the time. Remember the three youngsters Yogita Khatwani, a former airhostess along with her two friends driving up to the official residence of the Prime Minister, unmindful of the risk involved (Hindustan Times: August 11,2006). Hairstyle, trendy clothes, loud music, messy rooms are all a psychological need of growing up. It will be to the advantage of both, the parent and the child to understand this phenomenon. They are living life right down the middle with all the attendant land-mines. They haven't yet learnt to run a zig-zag pattern.

Remember! Discipline is not about exercising restriction: Your child needs to be disciplined. However, discipline does not mean restricting them. Disciplining means letting them behave properly so that they can become good persons.

You are not an adversary of the child. Therefore, it is **absolutely essential for parents to spend time with teenagers** in a friendly manner, help them by counselling and **guide them to set goals** for themselves to enable them to work in that direction. As they are pursuing their goal passionately, they are unlikely to go astray. They should also be guided towards leisure time pursuits, the finer points of life, like reading, singing, dancing, theatre, painting, playing an instrument etc. Adolescents with keen interest in a hobby are seen to become high achievers as it helps to re-energise them for studies.

Those youth who have not achieved anything in any field because of lack of parental attention and guidance begin to seek satisfaction out of sensational acts. If such a student of class XII is getting a kick out of seeing a movie at the multiplex, playing truant from the school today, tomorrow he will get a thrill only from drinking or smoking and day after tomorrow, only from drugs. It will not even stop here: he will then look for higher sensation: may be from BMW, Mercedes or a pistol or a gun — either of his own, borrowed or the stolen one. In such cases, limits have to be set. **We cannot shirk our parental responsibility.** If the behaviour or action of your child is going to harm him/her or somebody else, **put your foot down and keep it there:** otherwise let the teenager decide. **[The 16 yr. old boy allegedly driving the Honda Accord** at 200 km./hr. on Nelson Mandela Marg in

Delhi, critically injured a cyclist (H.T. 17.8.2006) is such an example. If the parents had not given the key of the car the accident would not have taken place. However, if parents continue to indulge in their children they should not repent if their wards become sociopaths. Try to recall the Jessica Lal, Priyadarshini Mattu murder cases.

Understand the age group: Your child passes through various stages; you should understand these ages and treat accordingly. Parenting a baby is different from parenting a toddler.

The child drifts away because **parents have not spared time for him/her.** Therefore, (s)he has gone somewhere else where **he/she was heard patiently.** We have ourselves alienated the child and passed on the power of influencing him elsewhere. Parents must give due recognition to the teenager by publicly honouring him for his achievements by way of announcing the same to friends, visitors, relatives, neighbours, etc. If parents look back at their own time of adolescence, they will realise that they have passed through the same vulnerability. But the situation is not irretrievable: it is never too late to start working on your son or daughter.

IF YOU THINK

If you think you are beaten, you are.

If you think you dare not, you don't!

If you like to win, but think you can't,

It's almost a cinch you won't.

If you think you'll lose, you're lost;

For out in the world we find

Success begins with a fellow's will;

It's all in the state of mind.

If you think you are outclassed, you are,

You've got to think high to rise,

You've got to be sure of yourself before

You can ever win a prize.

Life's battles don't always go

To the stronger and faster man,

But sooner or later the man who wins

Is the man who thinks he can?

Badness you can get easily, in quantity: the road is smooth and it lies close by. But in front of excellence the immortal gods have put sweat, and long and steep is the way to it, and rough at first: but when you come to the top, then it is easy.

-Hesiod, c.700 B.C., the Theogony

Parents and the School

Having given a broad idea about the nature and attributes of children of different ages, there are a few general things which one could keep in mind for the proper growth, academic achievement and grooming of the children. These suggestions are given below:

I. Get Involved in the School

I have seen children from ordinary families who flourished and progressed excellently because their parents supported them in their childhood. **Such parents consciously instil a positive image in the child:** an atmosphere of trust and encouragement exists. For such children we may not be able to measure the results, but it can definitely be felt. During my interaction with children, I have observed that most of them have above average intelligence.

The variance in accomplishments is generally directly proportional to the parental interest, encouragement and the importance of hard work and self-discipline instilled in the child. Studies also support the connection. Therefore, the parents must get involved with the child's school. When a note is received from the school in the child's diary, instead of getting irritated it is advisable to immediately respond and make it convenient to go and discuss the matter with the teacher. It proves to the teacher that you not only care for the child but have regard for the school as well and hence the teacher will also take equal interest in the child. The youngster too begins to feel that you are truly interested in him. It does not suffice to tell the child you love him but it has to be proved by action where the parents have to make genuine efforts.

Attend all the PTMs, School Functions, Get Together moments at school without fail. When both MOM and DAD go to school together, the kids love it!

We should never criticise the school, more so in the presence of the child. He must be given a positive image of the school and the teacher, for only then good and fast learning will take place. You will not be able to change the working of the institution. Your grumbling that the school is too strict or too lenient or it lays too much emphasis on studies or on co-curricular activities etc. **is not going to change the situation.** Instead, requests and suggestions be made: the child is bound to benefit. If you have a complaint, **try not to put the teacher on the defensive.** Approach the teacher in all humility with a co-operative spirit. Remember! both you and the teacher are interested in the welfare and progress of the child. She will definitely do whatever is humanly possible within the existing constraints.

The man who does not read good books has no advantage over the man who can't read.

- Mark Twain

Children Learn What They Live

If a child lives with criticism,

he learns to condemn.

If a child lives with praise,

he learns to appreciate.

If a child lives with hostility,

he learns to fight.

If a child lives with tolerance,

he learns to be patient.

If a child lives with ridicule,

he learns to be shy.

If a child lives with encouragement,

he learns confidence.

If a child lives with shame,

he learns to feel guilty.

If a child lives with approval,

he learns to like himself.

If a child lives with fairness,

he learns justice.

If a child lives with security,

He learns to have faith.

If a child lives with acceptance and friendship,

He learns to find love in the world.

II. Homework

These days it has become a fad especially with the 'elite' to decry the age-old practice of setting homework: from time to time some newspapers and magazines also castigate its usefulness. Here the argument is that the home is for home affairs, for a little chit-chat with the parents or for following other pursuits but they forget the advantages which accrue from doing the homework at home. Parents would do well to remember that the National Commission on Excellence in education in America cited lack of homework as one of the reasons American students have fallen behind those of other countries. Let me hasten to add that that is one of the main reasons for Indians doing exceedingly well in the world as they have developed the habit of working hard by organising themselves.

Homework should not be considered a sort of punishment or as a way of keeping the child busy and off our backs.

Teachers assign homework for:

1.　Re-inforcement of work done in the class.

2.　To get ready for the next day's class.

3.　To learn to use resources such as reference books, internet, encyclopedias etc.

4.　To get the in-depth knowledge in a particular subject, since neither the time in the class is sufficient nor the environment conducive.

The teacher explains the subject matter, children listen to her, take mental and written notes, do some work in the class and then complete it at home. They may do two sums in the school and 3-4 at home: I see nothing else in this except the child gaining mastery over the subject. There isn't just enough time in the class to do a detailed study of the subject matter. At home there is no time limit to reflect, practice and assimilate the topic at hand. Research has proved the common sense feeling that those who do the homework sincerely and revise from time to time, digest the subject matter better and score more than those who do not.

Homework is valuable for other reasons too. It teaches students self-discipline and self-direction, cultivates wholesome habits and attitudes and fosters initiative. It can encourage a life-long love for learning. Homework, in my opinion, is an extremely important component in the child's education. Studies have shown that carefully assigned and graded homework has greater influence on your child's academic success than any other factor like affluence, socio-economic status or educational background of the parents. Many educators, through their research work, have confirmed my firm conviction that the children flourish in an environment with exacting standards which includes clear expectations about homework.

Therefore, good homework habits should be instilled in the child from day one. A day's timetable be made specifically providing for homework but not ignoring aspects like games, hobbies, entertainment socialisation etc. **The greatest gift a parent can give to a child is to make him realise that learning is important and one of** the rules is to study at home as well. A reasonable quiet place which is well lit and away from the distraction of T.V. (better still if it is switched off) should be okay for the child to do his homework. The child be advised to carefully note down his homework in the school diary which the parents should see every evening and ensure that the child sits down to attend to the same as per the timetable. Writing Homework in the school almanac would also eliminate the time-wasting telephone calls to friends, finding out the same. Parents should ask the child to check the H.W. on the ERP if the school is following that practice.

Parents begin to think of homework as a burden as some of them mistakenly feel that they have to do it but that defeats the very purpose of homework. **They should encourage the child to attempt the homework on his own** and **minimal** help should be provided. The exact sum need not be done but a similar sum may be explained. Parents may help in memorising or other such areas of homework but **definitely not do it for them.** Parents are not experts in every subject and hence cannot be expected to help the child in all the subjects; their job is only to provide support and create an environment where child feels like attempting the homework. The homework cannot be perfect, nor do the teachers expect it to be; refinement takes place gradually.

Generally the homework varies as follows:

Grades	Duration/day
I _ III	20 - 60 minutes
IV _ VI	60 - 90 minutes
VII _ VIII	90 - 110 minutes

Thereafter students can devote time as per academic needs and the direction given by the school. As a guideline, the homework **should not exceed** 15 minutes multiplied by the class in which the child is studying.

The homework may be oral like learning spellings, or written or project work. There should be a **fixed duration** for doing the homework. Even if there is no homework the child be asked to review the work previously done or read some general books during the allotted time. This may discourage children from "forgetting" to bring home the assignments.

Elementary school students often like to have someone around at home while working on assignments. Many times they will have minor questions to ask and we should be available to help them to cross the hump. It will be a good idea that you yourself sit and do some reading or even make grocery list or the like while the child is engaged in attempting the homework. This will generate more interest in the child to persevere with the homework. **For deeper understanding of the subject matter, you may ask the child to teach you what (s)he has learnt as people learn best when they teach.**

III. Pocket Money

Those days, my mother gave me Rs. 5/-and made sure I was accountable for everything I did with it.

- Rohan Murthy (S/o Narayan Murthy)

Pocket money is a great way to help children learn the basics of managing money. But how much pocket money you give, when you give it and whether you give it at all depends on your family circumstances and values.

Pocket Money Basics: Giving pocket money to children as young as four or five years helps them start learning about **the value of money and money management.** For example, when children get pocket money, they have to make choices about spending or saving. If they're saving, they'll learn about waiting for things they want.

Pocket money can also help children learn about the **consequences** of losing money. Letting your children make a few mistakes _ like spending all their hard-earned savings on fake tattoos instead of a cricket set _ is part of the learning process.

It's OK to put limits on what your child spends his pocket money on. For example, you might discourage him from buying lollies if that interferes with his appetite for nutritious food or you want to protect his teeth from decay.

When to give children pocket money?

There are no hard and fast rules about when to start giving children pocket money.

Your child might be ready to try managing some pocket money if she understands that:

- she needs money to get things from shops

- it's **important to save money**, and not spend it all

- spending all her money today means there's no more until the next payment.

How much pocket money?

This depends on your circumstances and what you think is reasonable. As long as your child understands how much he'll get and how often, he can start learning how to use the money well.

You can base your decision about how much pocket money to give on:

- what household chores you expect your child to do

- what your family budget will allow

- how old your child is _ for example, you might give a five-year-old ₹10 per day and a seven-year-old ₹15 per day

- what you expect pocket money to pay for _ for example, if you expect it to cover things like lunches and savings, you might need to give much more.

What should pocket money cover?

Pocket money could cover any of the following things:

- saving for a special game or toy

- special outings like the movies

- gifts for siblings and extended family members

Tips on giving pocket money

Here are some pocket money tips:

- Explain to your child what the pocket money is meant for. For example, if pocket money is to cover entertainment or food, agree on what kinds of entertainment are OK. It might help to write a list.

- Negotiate guidelines about how much money can go into saving, spending and donating. For example, you and your child might agree that your child puts 50% of his pocket money into savings, 40% into spending and 10% into donating.

- Pay what you can afford, regardless of what other parents (or your child!) might say.

- Pay it on a set day. You might choose to pay daily, weekly, fortnightly or monthly.

- Set up jars to help your child divide her money _ for example, one jar for spending on small things she wants now and one for saving towards bigger things.

- Put saved money in a money box. As the level grows, it highlights the achievement of being a good saver.

- Try not to supplement pocket money or pay in advance _ it's all about teaching your child to spend no more than he earns.

Learning about money

Your child learns a lot by watching you and how you deal with money. Spending, saving or donating money _ they're all chances to teach your child more about the basics of money management.

As children get older, you can teach them about:

- **the value of money**: the relative price of things

- **spending**: accepting that money is gone once it's spent

- **earning**: understanding that earning money can be hard work, but usually that's the only way to get it

- **saving**: using short-term and long-term goals

- **investing**: learning that you have the chance to earn more when you invest

- **borrowing**: understanding the importance of repaying borrowed money

- **opportunity cost**: understanding that when you use money to buy something, you give up the chance to buy something else with that money.

(Source: raisingchildren.net)

In his wisdom Bishop Raju, head of schools run by church of North India, Kolkata, sent a circular in July, 2006 limiting the pocket-money of school-going children to maximum of Rs. 30 per day. I whole-heartedly subscribe to his views. It's a matter of great concern that some parents give huge amounts to their children to splurge, either in the school, or elsewhere. Since in middle-class families these days both mother and father are working, they feel guilty of not spending time with their children and hence they substitute the lack of time with liberal pocket- money. Parents should remember that children are not mature enough to handle unlimited amount of money. Parents should take care of their tiffin, birthday gifts to siblings and friends, buying of story-books and other such needs. If you notice, many of the consumer ads are directed towards growing up children, trying to catch them in their webs. But we must remember children need to be supervised and guided till they can differentiate right from wrong. Although the amount of pocket-money is a matter of family discussion, it is certain that loose money at the disposal of children will definitely lead them astray.

Teach your child the value of money: Money has a great importance in life, teach your children it is not easy to make money. If you are giving pocket money, check how they are spending.

Excessive pocket-money encourages children from uncaring families to flaunt their affluence which leads to undesirable activities, be it indiscipline, smoking, drinking, drugs or sexual misadventure etc. Therefore, it is suggested that limited pocket-money, as parents deem fit, be given to children for buying knick-knacks from the school canteen.

IV. Exams

> *Education is what survives when what has been learned has been forgotten.*
>
> **- B.F. Skinner**

Try and recall your own time when you were to sit for exams. They put a tremendous pressure on the mind of the child, sometimes making it a matter of life and death. Therefore, it is necessary for parents not only to understand but continuously help their children to **take exams in their stride.** Try and impress upon the child to be regular and study throughout the year rather than a month or two before the exams.

Small doses given regularly are definitely better than an overdose. What is required is to ensure that the child is regular to school and does the daily homework meticulously. Review of the work done earlier will ensure that the child has learnt it properly and will not be required to memorise and regurgitate. To reduce the pressure from the mind of the child, we as adults, should create an atmosphere at home whereby the child begins to think that the exams are a normal part of student life. Children are worth more than a mere percentage. A nerve-racking current runs through my spine when I see students competing for marks up to second place of decimal! Exams are not the end of the world. There is always a tomorrow. There is more to life than just marks. De-emphasise the importance of one shot exam. Most of the schools and the boards now insist on regular study rather than pressure cooker learning. Parents should help the child making a time-table so that the child can attend to his studies throughout the year on a daily basis. Exams are important but in the larger scheme of things they are a small part. Look back and see how much those marks and results have played a part in your life. During exam time, the adolescent is burdened with almost unbearable pain cognitively. Ensure that the normal routine of entertainment, casual talk at home, and activities continue, to avoid excessive pressure. It does not mean that the complete pressure be taken off: some stress is good to spur them to move forward, but care should be taken that the pot does not boil over.

However, till the examination system changes, I give below a few suggestions, which if implemented, will reduce exam stress among students. Parents should ensure:

1. The child prepares well; instil faith in him that he doesn't doubt himself.

2. He avoids comparison with others.

3. He keeps away from distractions.

4. Absorption of the subject is emphasised and cramming is

not in place throughout the year. Learning by rote generates nervousness.

5. The best way to remember is to picture what you have learnt. This can be done by closing your eyes and picturising the important points: it gets recorded on your mental tape.

6. **Mnemonics:** Another way of remembering is to associate the subject matter with some word, situation or a thing(s) e.g. **VIBGYOR, BODMAS** or After School to College or Add Sugar to Coffee for remembering the signs of trigonometrical ratios, in different quadrants. For learning the spellings of Attendance let the child remember **AT TEN DANCE** or for the spellings of Mathematics the child could associate with **MA THE MA TICS.** You can innovate many more such associations to augment the child's memory.

7. You will have to examine the learning style of your child. First, _Visual learning style:_ these children learn best when they read, write or see something like pictures of Heart, Eye, Volcano etc. Second, _Auditory learning style:_ these children learn faster by hearing. Parents can read to them, discuss with them, they may study together with friends and read to each other: Audio tapes can be used. Third, _Kinesthetic learning style:_ In this style children learn best through activities e.g., a skit or a short play on Akbar or Ashoka or Gandhi would ensure excellent learning. Experimentation, Field Trips and Project Work will yield encouraging results for such children.

These are not clearly demarcated styles, they merge into each other but each child gains the maximum from the method he prefers. When we hear we can recall about 30 per cent of the matter, when we read we can recall 35 to 40 per cent, when we see, about 50 per cent can be recalled and when we tell somebody, memory retains around 60 per cent and it increases to 75 per cent when we do it (or write it). **Therefore, it is advised that we help the child to use all senses to learn for excellent** results. Let the child not despair; he should do his best and I can assure your life will bring him the best.

> *There is so much good in worst of us,*
> *and so much bad in the best of us,*
> *that behaves all of us,*
> *not to talk about the rest of us.*
>
> *- Stevenson*

हार नहीं होती

लहरों से डर कर नौका पार नहीं होती।
कोशिश करने वालों की कभी हार नहीं होती।।

नन्हीं चीटी जब दाना लेकर चलती है।
चढ़ती दीवारों पर, सौ बार फिसलती है।।

मन का विश्वास रगों में साहस भरता है।
चढ़कर गिरना, गिरकर चढ़ना न अखरता है।।

आखिर उसकी मेहनत बेकार नहीं होती।
कोशिश करने वालों की कभी हार नहीं होती।।

डुबकियाँ सिंधु में गोताखोर लगाता है।
जा–जा कर खाली हाथ लौटकर आता है।।

मिलते न सहज ही मोती गहरे पानी में।
बढ़ता दूना उत्साह इसी हैरानी में।।

मुट्ठी उसकी खाली हर बार नहीं होती।
कोशिश करने वालों की कभी हार नहीं होती।।

असफलता एक चुनौती है, स्वीकार करो।
क्या कमी रह गई, देखो और सुधार करो।।

जब तक न सफल हों, नींद, चैन को त्यागो तुम।।
संघर्षों का मैदान छोड़, मत भागो तुम।।

कुछ किए बिना ही जय–जयकार नहीं होती।
कोशिश करने वालों की कभी हार नहीं होती।।

—हरिवंश राय बच्चन

They who provide much wealth and resources

for their children, but neglect to improve them

in virtue, do like those who feed their horses

high, but never train them to be useful.

-Socrates

The woods are lovely, dark and deep,

But I have promises to keep

And miles to go before I sleep,

And miles to go before I sleep.

-Robert Frost

Family life is its own way

of training the young,

and homes are very much

what family makes them.

-Smiles

Home Life

I. United Front

Jean Piaget, the famous Swiss psychologist, has argued that **people actively manipulate the objects and events around them.** Children too take advantage of the father pitted against the mother, parents and the grandparents. You must have seen this happening in your family. Sometimes it leads to parental conflict also. Therefore, it is suggested that the **father and mother, parents and grandparents put up a united front** for proper grooming of the child. This need not happen on every issue. However, you and your spouse must come to an agreement in private and then communicate the decision to the child.

In many families it is an established norm that the mother will not finally decide but ask the child to wait till the father returns home. This is a very wise practice and should be continued. Also parents should establish early contact with the teacher for the child to understand that he cannot play one against the other. In addition the teacher will know the background of the family and parents will remain in touch with the progress of the child.

I have observed that when the parents and teacher know each other, the teacher naturally pats, encourages and gives positive strokes to the child. With this type of encouragement, automatically the child's progress will be better and swifter.

UNITY

I dreamed I stood

in a studio

And watched two

sculptors there

The clay they used

Was a young child's mind

And they fashioned

It with care

One was a teacher

The tools she used

Were books and music and art:

One was a parent

With a guiding hand

And a loving heart.

And when at last

Their work was done

They were proud of

What they had wrought

For the things they

Had worked into the child

Could never be sold or bought

And each agreed she

would have failed

if she had worked alone

For behind the parent stood the school

And behind the teacher

Stood the home.

-R.A. Lingenfelter

II. Intelligent Handling

I can vividly recall the case of Hemant Ahuja, the child aged $3^{1/2}$ years, (now married and a full-fledged engineer) who was being interviewed for admission to nursery class. The Headmistress asked the child to recite a nursery rhyme. But he was unwilling to do so. Psychological handling was required because she felt that the child was intelligent but was not in a mood to interact. The Headmistress immediately asked the child whether he would recite the Nursery rhyme to a frog. He readily agreed. We had a small nature-pond in the school and Hemant was immediately taken there and shown the frog. To her delight, the child recited the nursery rhyme happily.

I was much pleased to see Dr. Gupta, a pediatrician, handling a child, called Nandini, of about $4^{1/2}$ years of age. An injection was to be given but Nandini was scared of the prick. The doctor understood the situation and asked Nandini whether she would object to giving the injection to a duck. Obviously she agreed. The doctor drew the outline of a duck on her thigh and injected the dose. The child was happy and the job was done satisfactorily.

When our daughter Tisca (of Tare Zameen Par fame) was about 8 yrs of age, she would wake up at night with some kind of fear. It continued for 3-4 nights and we got much concerned. We thought of handling it psychologically. We are not superstitious parents but as a tactical move we told her that by keeping a metallic object under one's pillow the fear disappears: we also narrated her a couple of cooked up stories where by doing so the fear had vanished from the lives of those children. So, we gave her a stainless steel spoon to put under her pillow before going to bed which she willingly did. Lo and behold! Her fear disappeared in a few days and never recurred.

The important point I am trying to make is that sometimes **straightforward methods do not achieve what intelligent handling easily accomplishes.** Parents have to think of innovative ideas to tackle the situation. The age-old method of diverting the attention of the child by changing the topic in diffusing the situation is always helpful. Some of the other ways are redirection, facial gestures, proximity to the child, tone of voice (loving or firm voice) humour, etc.

> *We speak of educating our children: do we know that our children also educate us?* **- Sigourney**

III. Enlarge the Scope of Learning

It is not enough to tell the child 'A' stands for an apple. By using some imagination, through an apple, a child can be made to learn much more. Ask the child to feel it; show him the peel and the seeds: He can learn the words cut, taste, slice, piece, circle, sphere, oval, crescent, thin, thick, big, small, green, red, pink, hard and soft. With a little more initiative the parents can ask the child to sow the seed and can provide the pleasure to the child of experiencing how the seed changes into a sapling and a sapling into a plant. Of course, the knowledge and experience being given has to be age specific.

Most children are fond of ice-cream but we as parents miss out an excellent opportunity to provide a learning experience. One could tell the child about different flavours, cold, cool, milk, cream, freeze, melt, lick, mouth, tongue, hold, sweet, favourite, cup, cone, etc.

From the above examples, it is clear that **parents can lead the child onto concepts as well** e.g. big, small; thin, thick; light, heavy; cold, hot; solid, liquid; wet, dry. There are umpteen instances in daily life  from where the concept of long short; bright, dull; rough, smooth etc. can be passed on to the child without putting unnecessary pressure: At a later stage of growth, the child could be shown the experiment of air pressure by making use of the desert cooler, power of the steam can be understood by observing the lid of a sauce-pan rattle up and down when the water boils or noticing the steam coming out with force from the pressure cooker. He can be shown experiments on convertibility e.g. two equal juice packs be taken in two straight glasses of the same size. The contents of one could be poured into a broader glass and the child could be asked which was more. Straightaway the child would tell us that the contents in the first glass are more which obviously is not true: by pouring the contents back, the child would realise the concept of convertibility. Similarly, the concept of conversion of mass could be brought home to the child.  Principles of reflection and refraction, image is as far behind as the object in front of the mirror etc. can be pointed out as they occur in daily life. Although these concepts may not be learnt by the child immediately, it will become a part of his passive ideas to be easily understood later in life. **The child should be encouraged to estimate, predict, draw inference, etc.** A child' environment offers many practical opportunities to learn: **once we become conscious that the potential is there in situations** we can exploit the same and give our children a firm practical understanding around which theoretical knowledge can be built later.

IV. Create a Learning Atmosphere

Often I have seen the parents move heaven and earth to get their child admitted in a 'good' school, although I don't really understand what their idea of 'good' is! They would do well to remember that it is not enough to put the child in a well-known

school. Even the so called 'good' schools haven't invented any potion to turn out 'brilliant' persons. Learning does not end with a degree or a diploma. To me, it's a way of life. **Children will pick up those habits that they see at home or in their social circle.**

If children see us reading books, consulting a dictionary or encyclopedia or surfing the Internet, they will themselves feel motivated to adopt the same approach. It is through the environment that they are drawn to learning in a positive manner and for its own sake. Some suitable age relevant magazines could be subscribed to and placed on the shelf: there could be some story-books suitable for children; it has tremendous impact on a young mind. **We should start reading stories to our children from an early age. While reading we should give voice to the characters to capture the imagination of the child.** Our effort should be to make the written word come alive. Active reading stimulates language development and encourages independent thinking and develops imagination. We should ask relevant questions from the story. This will ignite their thinking further. It gives a head-start to the child in his education.

Admit your mistakes: When you admit your mistakes, your children will learn to apologize when they commit wrongs. Admitting your mistakes in front of your child will not diminish your personality.

Therefore, get your child hooked on to reading and its joy and relaxation will be life-long. I vividly remember the case of Nikhil, the son of Mr. Juneja, a friend of mine. Whenever Mr. Juneja read an interesting article in a magazine or a newspaper which was suitable for his teenager he would ask his son to read the same. Nikhil could never say no to his father and would read the clippings. They would sit together in the evening and discuss the same. In addition to concretizing Nikhil's ideas, it developed in him a taste for reading. So much so, that during his college days he started contributing articles to a youth magazine and in the bargain earned plenty of pocket-money. This was a subtle way on the part of Mr. Juneja to inculcate the habit of reading in his son.

Focus on your child's interests. When learning engages children in areas and subjects of interest, learning becomes fun and children engage in learning happily. If you really want to help your child to become a good learner, encourage him to explore topics and subjects that fascinate him. If he likes dinosaurs, help him find engaging and interesting books and stories about dinosaurs. Then challenge him to identify his five favorite dinosaurs and explain why he chose each one.

There could be a small library at home. It need not be expensive. Low priced NBT, CBT books for children are available. One could exchange books with friends. One can even buy used books at throwaway prices from pavements booksellers or other such places. For small children, books with pictures and bold type with very few words on each page be selected. At this age, they like the stories to be read to them. As they grow older, their reading tastes change and they may begin to like books on affection, kindness, friendship, concern for animals, stories with morals etc. From about 9 years onwards they pass on to books on adventure, mystery, detective novels, boarding school stories and the little pranks, feasts, picnics of boarders, Amarchitra katha etc. Stories by R.K. Narayan and Ruskin Bond also begin to attract the attention of children of age group 9-12 yrs. Harry Potter books by J.K. Rowling also catch their imagination. They begin to take interest in nature, space, sea world, inventions and discoveries, Tell Me Why, Tell Me How series, Rudyard Kipling's Kim, Enid Blyton's Famous Five and Secret Seven series. Nancy Drew books also capture their imagination. Scholastic has brought out interesting books for children.

Give them books: Books are an abundant source of knowledge. Encourage children to read books. When they are reading, pick up your book and sit with them reading your book.

Some of the suggested books/Series with their authors/ publications are given below:

Age Group: 3 - 6 Yrs

Any Touch and Feel, Scratch and Sniff, Pop-up or Lift and Learn books by Darling Kindersley or Scholastic or Himkler would whet your child's reading appetite. 'Read with me' series of Lady Bird is also good for this age group. Books by Eric Carle, Allan Ahlesberg would also interest the child. Topsy and TIm books would also catch the imagination of the tiny tots. Parents could read one chapter every evening as a bedtime story. It will be a good signal for children to wind down: it develops a bond between parent and child, sharpens the listening skills and increases concentration.

Age Group: 6-9 Yrs

Books	Authors	Publications
Favourite Tales (Series)	—	Lady Bird
Noddy Books	Enid Blyton	
Disney's Winnie the Pooh series	A. Milne	Egmonth

My little story teller (series)	—	Tiny Tot
Collection of small stories	Enid Blyton	Award Publication
		Children Book Trust

Ronald Dahl, Dr. Seuss and Dick King Smith books are also recommended for this age group.

Age Group: 9-12 Yrs

Books	Authors	Publications
Series of Great Illustrated Classics in Abridged form	—	—
Famous Five series	Enid Blyton	Hodder Children's book
Secret Seven Series	Enid Blyton	Hodder Children's books
Mystery Series	Enid Blyton	Mammoth
Hardy Boys Series	Franklin W. Dixon	Aladdin Paperback
Nancy Drew Series	Carolyn Keene	Aladdin Paperback
Harry Potter Series	J.K. Rowling	Bloomsbury Paperback
Time Machine	H.G. Wells	Pearson Prentice Hall

Treasure Island, Moby Dick and the Chronicles of Namia by C.S. Lewis are also suggested for pre-teens.

Read aloud to children: You can encourage reading habit by reading aloud to your children. You read a paragraph and then ask your child to read. Children love to listen to their parents. Reading together creates a bonding.

12 Yrs onwards: Self Help books, Inspirational books, light romance stories, Princess Diaries, Ruskin Bond, Charlie and the Chocolate Factory and The Witches by Ronald Dahl, The Flight of the Falcon by Daphne Du Maurier are interesting books for teenagers. Once they develop the habit of reading then they are on their own and can look for books themselves.

Sometimes when you ask the child to read a book (s) he may not feel like reading but will show great enthusiasm if the book is recommended by an older friend. Parents should take advantage of this suggestion as it works very well.

V. Share Time with Children

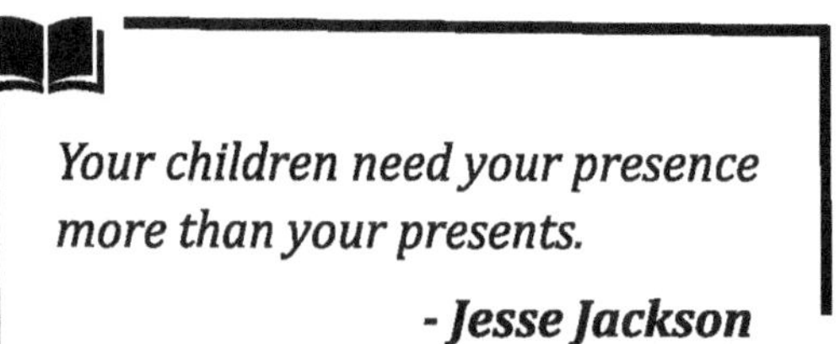

If the working parents return home at 6:00 p.m. and rush for their answering machine, start checking their emails or messages on WhatsApp or begin making business telephone calls, the child is bound to feel neglected and go astray. We may not realise but children do understand where the priority lies. It is important that we attend to them, talk about their school matters, friends and activities: we must ask how they bruised their elbow or hurt their ankle: we should keep an eye on them with a view to guide. **They will not learn from sermons, but certainly from our own examples.** While casually talking we should throw a seminal idea, drop a hint, give some examples where somebody has been honest, shown compassion and tolerance and has been rewarded or point out from current happenings the mean deeds of some people who have been reprimanded or punished by society or law or Nature. Gradually, they will realise that good actions are commended and reprobation held out either by Man or by Nature. Other examples of hard-working people who have achieved something worthwhile in life could be brought to the notice of children to emulate. Advice given incidentally will settle like snow, softly and firmly, but do's and don'ts hurt. It is important that the whole family sits together in an informal manner whether it is munching peanuts or shelling peas or eating a meal together with the T.V. switched off. The idea is that children come out with their problems or worries and solutions are found. An effort should be made to involve the children in discussions, ask their opinion and make them a part of decision making.

VI. Play Together, Stay Together

Spend quality time: In order to understand your child, you should spend quality time. If you spend quality time you will also develop a friendship bond with your child.

Viewing of T.V., computer games and mobile phones leave very little time for intra-family communication. Indoor games are one of the excellent ways of bonding with your children. Normally we do a reality check: Have you done your homework? Have you taken your Chyavanprash? But we rarely sit together and enjoy. If the whole family joins to play a game of Snakes and Ladders, Ludo, Chess, Scrabble or Boggle or Carrom, the children begin to see parents not just authority figures but as equals. These games foster camaraderie. Remember fun is a great equaliser. In addition children not only learn to share, play with honour, to lose with grace but **also get training in survival skills.** They overcome the temptation of cheating and **learn to play the game of life by the whistle.** Therefore, it is desirable that you fit fun into your schedule with children.

This will generate a tension-free atmosphere at home, congenial for proper development. **This sit down family ritual is a time when values, morals, attitudes are automatically**

absorbed by children. It is absolutely necessary to offset the appalling language and behaviour children are exposed to on T.V. and in movies. We should at suitable moments, condemn the arrogant and crude characters emphasising that good families do not indulge in such things. Real life is different from reel life!

When books are opened and read, you discover you have wings.

-Halen Hayes

The best school of education is discipline at home.

-Smiles

Remembering the Children

Let the children sing,

Let the children dance,

Let the children play,

In a safe and joyful way.

And teach them how to pray.

Let the children walk,

Let the children talk,

To friends, relatives, parents.

Show them all nature's wealth

Let them relate to its health.

Let the children work

At chores selected to fulfill

Full use of energies and will

To complete, to give and enact

The meaning of commitment

Let the children read

Everything within their reach,

All the things that teach,

And when there's peace within

There'll be peace without.

- Hildred Majorie Schloss

VII. Exposure

Children should be given the maximum "exposure. They should be taken to the nearby museum, zoo, children's theatre, exhibitions, art galleries, dance recitals etc. At a later stage, they should see places of historical interest, artistic beauty, famous places of worship etc: they should travel, for it widens the mental horizon: they should go trekking, camping, hiking etc. **Involvement in co-curricular activities sharpens the intellectual, social, cultural and physical talents.** However, if the scholastic achievement is to remain high, these pursuits should not become an end in themselves.

Provide your child opportunities: Let your child explore his hobbies, interests, and skills by providing opportunities.

Opportunities could be provided to them to meet people of eminence and integrity. Gradually we should ensure that they do not remain in awe of the greatest and the mightiest, for **everybody has feet of clay!** Even when programmes are being watched on television, one could engage the children in intelligent discussion which will concretize their ideas and develop the habit of thinking.

VIII. Self-Learning

We as parents should not volunteer the information to children immediately but lead them onto finding the information. Together, we should look up, search and find answers. Instead of giving the name of the capital of Japan, we could ask the child to look up the atlas or go to the internet from where he will discover not only the name of Tokyo but also many more things about the city. Moreover, he will be tempted to read about many other countries. **There is not only great pleasure in discovering things for oneself but also one retains the information for a longer period.** Piaget's findings confirm this when he writes "each time one prematurely teaches a child something he could have discovered for himself, that child is kept from inventing it and consequently from understanding it completely". Scared learning is no learning: **rote learning amounts to becoming a carbon copy. Real learning takes place through seeing, hearing, exploration, experimenting, making mistakes and finally arriving at correct things. The ultimate aim is learning to learn.**

> *"Self-education is, I firmly believe,*
> *the only kind of education there is."*
> **- Isaac Asimov**
>
> *"I never give answers.*
> *I lead from one question to another.*
> *That is my leadership."*   **- Tagore**

Let them learn: You are certainly more knowledgeable than your child, but your child is not ignorant, he has his own ntelligence. Let him learn things in his own ways. The more they learn the more they get out of their life.

I can vividly recall my days at the University of Bristol, U.K. I chose to study at this university for my PGCE qualification chiefly because it was not a one shot examination course. Through satisfactory attendance at lectures and tutorials, completion of course-work and the writing of a number of essays, one could obtain one's PGCE, in effect, one's license to teach. When the course began, I discovered that life was not as simple as I had imagined. I, and my equally naive colleagues, tackled the first of a series of essays by reading a recommended book, which consisted of some two hundred closely printed pages. And there, at the end, was given a select list "for further reading'. Another book had to be tackled with, as you may have guessed, the same injunction at the end: 'for further reading'! All-in-all, I must have read half-a-dozen books with care and assiduous note-taking in order to produce that first essay. And there were many more essays to follow!

This is how learning took place at the University of Bristol. In order to excel we had to work, and consequently ploughed our way through many more books, periodicals, reference works, case studies, etc. than would be expected from a graduate who pursued an examination-oriented course of study. The candidate who single-mindedly studies to pass would most probably cram a few important questions by rote-learning so as to regurgitate the same in the examination hall, and immediately thereafter forget the contents, let alone their application. That is no learning! But since we were active participants in selecting what educational material we assimilated, not only were we motivated partners in learning, but all that we learned was relevant and of real significance to us.

That is where I realized how real learning takes place. It is with directed exploration, experimentation and observation, and with considerable amount of reflection by both the student and the teacher. Rabindranath Tagore did not go to a formal school. He was a self-taught man learning everything at his father's library. He was the very epitome of **self-learning** as he went on to win the Nobel Prize. Sachin Tendulkar kept refining his skills of batting throughout his career. He is considered one of the greatest batsmen living today.

Learning takes place when one is internally motivated with a desire to gain knowledge or a skill, or even attitudes in the societal context. For example, starting as a class IV employee, the former Chief Justice of India Honourable Sarosh Homi Kapadia rose to be Chief Justice of India, all by **self-learning**. Therefore, I strongly feel children should be encouraged to learn for themselves by reading, through assimilating, thinking, discussing with seniors and peers and project work. Unlimited potential for learning is embedded in us humans and given a stimulating and enabling atmosphere, children can transform into lifelong learners. Our job as parents and teachers is to act as catalyst, create conducive environment for learning and unlock their full potential.

Let the child be free: The thinking that you are his parent and you will never harm him has given birth to the thought that you should control your kids. Too much control is bad.

IX. Sanctions and Punishment

Most of the parents of today tend to believe that they are doing a particular deed (sanctions, punishment, etc.) or applying a certain disciplinary methodology for the good of the child itself. They also feel that the day will come when the child will appreciate them for all the punishment, telling them that had they not inflicted punishment on him, he would not have been the person he is today, or would not have tasted the fruits of success.

But, the irrefutable fact is that all these disciplinary actions, punishments prove to be more disservice than good. These (actions) create irreparable damage or negative impact on child's self-esteem.

Punishment only scares the young child: He/she also begins to think that punishment is the only method of tackling things. Better method for correcting him/her is to impose sanctions_ withdrawing of privileges *i.e.,* we can temporarily withdraw our affection like kissing Goodnight before sleeping or curtailing the play time to half or not allowing the child to view for a day his/her favourite programme on the T.V. Older children may rebel against punishment e.g. A boy, Sanjeev Duggal, of class XII broke the lid of a cistern in the toilet by placing a cracker inside it, during Diwali time. An enquiry was held and the culprit nailed down. His name was announced so that others were deterred from indulging in such acts of rowdyism. He was made to pay the cost of two lids to ensure that he learns a lesson. The resentment remained in his mind but he could not do anything as he was helpless. However, when he had received the Admittance Card (Roll. No.) for the board examination, he broke two more lids! It dawned on me that crude punishment does not have the corrective effect.

On the other hand counselling and advice help, as illustrated by the case of Nitish Narang, a student of Class XII. He was brought to me by a teacher for not behaving well in the class. It was a minor incident and did not require dealing with deeply as I knew that the teacher was incompetent both subject-wise as well as personality-wise. However, I had to support the teacher and hence advised the child to behave well and concentrate on his studies. Both of them went back to the class. After about two hours, the boy returned to my office and enquired why I had not punished him. I explained that I had already advised him and no further action was required. It appeared that the matter had ended but lo and behold! The boy came to me again the next morning and requested for punishment. I understood immediately that the matter was weighing heavily on his mind and he wanted it to be done with.

Make punishment the last option. Punishment should be used only when all methods of behavioural management have failed.

I spent five minutes with him explaining how his life would improve by observing **self-discipline and remaining focused on the work at hand.** To my great pleasure, Nitish improved tremendously and passed with flying colours. The whiplash of conscience worked wonders with his psyche. Even after having left the school, he continues to visit me from time to time. Upon enquiry, he explained that he comes for renewal of inspiration!

Another method of dealing with adolescents is to channelise their energies. I can recall a class XI student, Samar Khan, who was always getting into trouble, either bullying small children or indulging in pranks, overstepping limits of discipline. His parents were called many times but to no avail. He was on the verge of being thrown out of school. However, I consulted the senior staff and we diverted his energy into debating. The result was nothing short of miraculous; his energies were fully channeled: not only did he get out of trouble but became the All India Best Debater. My heart swells with pride when I often see him on the television interviewing film stars with elan! This is a learning experience for us also as teachers/parents that we should try and find out what the child is good at and then channelise his energy in that direction.

X. Self-Esteem

Nobody holds a good opinion of a man who has a low opinion of himself.
- Anthony Trollope

Kids who feel good about themselves have the confidence to try new things. They are more likely to try their best. They feel proud of what they can do. Self-esteem helps kids cope with mistakes. It helps kids to try again, even if they fail at first. As a result, self-esteem helps kids to perform better at school, at home, and with friends.

Kids with low self-esteem feel unsure of themselves. If they think others won't accept them, they may not join in. They may let others treat them poorly. They may have a hard time standing up for themselves. They may give up easily, or not try at all. Kids with low self-esteem find it hard to cope when they make a mistake, lose, or fail. As a result, they may not do as well as they could.

(Source: kidshealth.org)

Isaac Newton had a low self-image at school. One day when the school bully hit him, he hit him back and the bully was knocked down. Newton's classmates appreciated this and he felt nice about himself. His self-esteem had gone up. He learnt to believe in himself. He improved in studies also.

My experience tells me that if we label children as dull, bad, unintelligent, slow, hyper, not able to achieve anything, they begin to *feel that way* and live up to the tag fixed on them. Criticism can result in overly self-critical child who will always be in doubt and fear to take risks. If the child keeps harping on his imagined weaknesses, they solidify as facts in his mind. A negative label can be a self-fulfilling prophecy. On the contrary, if we keep reinforcing that they belong to the family of achievers, or are students of an excellent school, they are capable of achieving outstanding results, they begin to take themselves as such. A brief, kind comment **"good work"**, **"intelligently done"** can work wonders. The confidence grows and hence achievement. If children have high self-esteem *i.e.,* how good they feel about themselves, then they begin to accept responsibility and aspire for high results: they think they **can** and hence they **do** achieve. If they are low in self-image they would not desire to achieve and will always look for outside validation whereas those who perceive themselves as worthwhile, will be internally motivated and do not need outside applause. If parents have faith in the abilities of their children from early childhood then the same belief gets passed on to the children.

Do not hurt his self-esteem: Your child is a distinct individual, he has his self-esteem. You don't want anyone to hurt your self-respect, do you?

Constant words of encouragement empower the child. Legitimate praise does wonders to the power of hearing and the personality of the child. It has a Pygmalion effect *i.e.,* if we keep reinforcing that they are good or useless they will begin to see themselves that way and hence live up to that level as the Cockney flower girl Eliza Dolittle turned into a high class lady in 'My Fair Lady'. I remember when I was doing my B.A. (Hons.) Ist year, my professor, Mr. Bhalla, while checking our précis, mentioned that my piece was 'well done'. This put me on to my life-long interest in English. The quality of self-respect should be inculcated from early childhood. "You could not have done it", you cannot lower yourself to this extent' etc. are cautionary messages for developing this characteristic. Self-esteem keeps us away from self destruction: it prevents children from cheating, breaking laws and hence protects them from **getting tempted to transient pleasures.** Behind all the success, accomplishments, glory and greatness lies the mountain-moving power of **belief in one's own powers.**

I am reminded of a parable whose moral is self-evident. A farmer put a pumpkin, as it was taking shape, in a small jar for no reason at all except to see what happens: while the other pumpkins grew in size, this particular pumpkin could grow only to the size of the jar and no more! **So don't limit the child.** Silence their gremlins_limiting beliefs which sabotage the harmonious growth and achievement of the child. Peer pressure, anti social elements and the media are constantly seducing children to engage in harmful habits like drugs, eating junk food, demeaning relationships, etc. Therefore, they be raised in an environment that fosters self-esteem for which they must be taught to value themselves. Hence, it is absolutely necessary that **we boo them as little as possible and cheer them as frequently as we can.**

XI. Role Model

> *Cheldren have never been very good at listening to their elders but they have never failed to imitate them.*
>
> ***- James Baldwin, Nobody knows my name***

One of the most powerful ways children learn what to do and what not to do is by watching us. Children cannot help but imitate us. Imperceptibly, we pass on our attitudes and feelings to our children. Even if we do not directly communicate our fears or complexes, children pick up the same through our emotional reaction e.g. it is in my experience that many mothers give a shriek when they see a cockroach, a mouse or a lizard or are scared of darkness, height and/or water. Their children will also be scared of the same things. If a husband hits his wife or the wife tells the husband to shut up or both together criticise a relative or swear at the neighbour they cannot expect their children's behaviour to be any better.

Become a role model: If you want your kid to be good, you should be a good person yourself. The kids are always watching you, never do anything bad more so in front of them.

Vulgar letters full of filth were found in the school bag of Aditi, a Class VIII student. Investigations revealed that she had written letters to herself. Later in a meeting with the mother it came as a shock to us that Aditi's father used to read pornographic material and these magazines were kept in their toilet. Aditi would sneak there and cut nude pictures and put them up on the display board in the school. The mother was ashamed but could not help as her husband would not mend his ways. On the other hand, most children learnt good manners, grace and magnanimity from their parents. The emotional reactions or practical situations get ingrained in the mind of the child. If you indulge in corrupt practices or watch excessive T.V. or go to kitty parties or gamble or approve permissiveness, or ask the child to tell a minor lie like to make your child convey to your friend that you are not at home despite being very much there, or obtain a false medical certificate for applying for leave, the child, as he takes things at face value, will subconsciously internalise the same. **When the spring is contaminated so will the water be.** Parenting is not merely laying down rules; it is playing by the rules also. **If you fudge on truth so will they.** If you are honest, polite, self-disciplined so will they be. Incidents conveying moral values, aspirations, courage, human relationships, sharing, caring and respect for elders narrated with feelings would have the desired effect on children. **Parents must become aware of their tremendous power to affect their child's attitudes like confidence, courage, compassion, tolerance etc.** I am afraid it is possible only if we as adults practice these attitudes ourselves in life.

"I learnt from my parents that it is important to live everyday of one's life with grace and honour... My father always encouraged me and told my mother that he had full faith in me...As I got older I felt I could not misuse that trust. He warned me against taking short cuts."

-Sachin Tendulkar

Do I need to stress that the seeds of good or bad thoughts, actions, moral and human values are sown at home. That is what we call **Sanskars**—culture of the family.

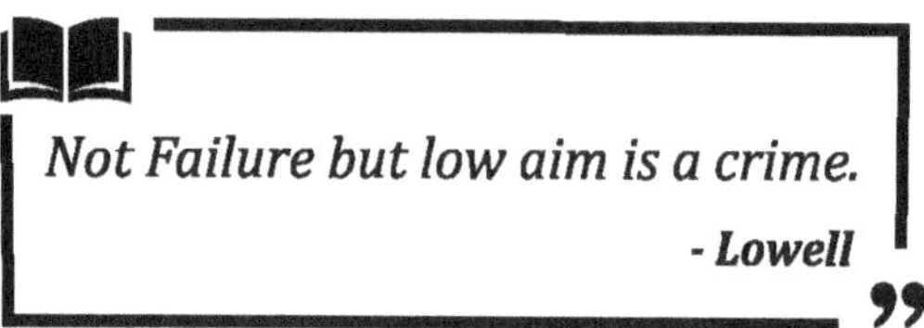

Children

Your children are not your children

They are the sons and daughters of life's longing for itself.

They come through you but not from you,

and though they are with you, yet they belong not to you.

You may give them your love but not your thoughts.

For they have their own thoughts.

You may house their bodies but not their souls,

for their souls dwell in the house of tomorrow,

Which you cannot visit, not even in your dreams.

You may strive to be like them,

but seek not to make them like you.

For life goes not backward nor tarries with yesterday.

You are the bows from which your children

as living arrows are sent forth.

The archer sees the mark upon the path of the infinite, and he bends you with his might that his arrows may go swift and far.

Let your bending in the archer's hand be for gladness;

for even as he loves the arrow that flies,

so he loves also the bow that is stable.

-Khalil Gibran

You get what you focus your time and energy on...If you focus mostly on limitation, those are what you experience: if you focus mostly on abundance and prosperity, you will, you must, experience those in your life. It is the universal law.

-John Cali

Suggested Activities

Some activities are being suggested below. These will not only make the child alert, observant, sharp and a thinking person but also sociable: in addition it will generate a relaxed atmosphere at home. Parents can think of many more such activities and enjoy with their sons and daughters.

1. Read to your child regularly. Ask questions about the stories read to him. Use the story to improve his vocabulary.

2. Memorise nursery rhymes, good songs, hymns, bhajans and sing them together at home, while cooking or doing domestic chores and even in parks or family outings, in fact anywhere.

3. Hide an object in a room and provide clues by clapping to help him locate the object. The faster the clapping the nearer he gets to the object.

4. Play number games like counting by deleting multiplies of 3 or 5 or 7.

5. Play with the digits of the number plates on cars e.g. adding, subtracting, multiplying, observing order, comparing numbers of different cars, observing symmetry viz. 3773: the reversibility in words like Mum, Dad, Deed, level, Solos, Madam, Arora, Nitin, Redder,

Malayalam (Palindrome): let them notice the names of shops, show them the beauty in trees, birds etc.

6. **Word Building:** The child speaks a letter say M, you add a letter say O, then the child adds N, you add K, the child adds E, you add Y. An effort should be made to ensure that the word does not end on the self. The word should have stopped at K-Monk. You actually lost at K.

7. **To Spy with an Eye:** While travelling you tell the child 'I spy with my eye' B: the child has to speak some word with B which is visible e.g. Bus. Then the child says 'I spy with my eye' S: you have to show him anything starting with S e.g. shop. A variation of this game can be speaking rhyming words like man, ran; ten, hen; can, ran, ban; air, hair, chair, care, player, mare, dare; etc.

8. **The Simon Game:** Explain to the child that an order will be given. He is to obey only when Simon orders *i.e.* if you tell the child, stand up, he should not stand up but when Simon says 'stand up' he should stand up otherwise he is out. You take turns playing the game.

9. **Pick the odd one:** Sofa, Chair, Table, Clock, Curtains, Towel.

10. Two similar pictures can be shown with minor differences. The child can be asked to point out the differences. Many such pictures are given in children's magazines.

11. Kim's Game:

    - You show the child 7-8 common things for 30 seconds.

    - Cover them, ask the child to name them. Take turns.

    - Things could be written also and then the child is asked to recall.

    - The child can be shown the grocery items in the cupboard and then see how many he can recall.

12. Depending upon the age the child be asked to read instructions on containers, packets of food, medicines, bottles, etc. These arouse more interest and are greater fun than the textbooks.

13. Language and mathematical crossword puzzles. Lots of them are given in supplements of Saturday, Sunday newspapers and also in may magazines.

14. Supplying the missing numbers in sequences like 3, 8, 13, 18, _____________; 4, 12, 36, 108, _______________.

15. Observe the pattern and fill in the blank e.g.

    5*4=23, 7*3=24, 8*5=...... .

16. Show/Perform simple scientific experiments: e.g. observe scientific phenomena:

    (i)   Power of steam   (ii)   Evaporation

    (iii) Condensation   (iv)   Distillation

    (v)   Reflection   (vi)   Refraction

    (vii) Air Pressure   (viii) Friction

    (ix)   Gravity etc.

17. Ask the child to play the role of a (i) Doctor (ii) Space scientist (iii) Pilot (iv) Prime Minister (v) Chief Justice (vi) Sometimes (s)he becomes the father/mother and you the son/daughter etc.

18. **Person of the Day:** Whenever a member of the family achieves something worthwhile (More than 80% marks, winning a match etc.) (s)he becomes the important person of the day. Within reasonable limits, his/her orders will prevail that day. (We have done it in our family with highly rewarding results.)

19. The child will benefit if the whole family sits together and prays. It brings down any existing tensions and creates a peaceful atmosphere. This ritual should be made so strong that it has to take place under any circumstances. It can come about when this practice

begins from the early years of the child.

More things are wrought by prayer than this world dreams of.

-Alfred, Lord Tennyson

The Idylls of the Kings

The same thing happened today that happened yesterday, only to different people. **- Walter Winchell**

Research Findings

In America research was conducted about teaching and learning during the time of President Ronald Reagan. The research findings, mainly reinforcement of common sense, were printed and distributed to parents all over U.S.A. for the benefit of their children. Briefly, the findings are given below:

1. The best way for parents to help their children become better readers is to read to them aloud_even when they are very young. Discuss the stories and talk about the meaning of words; ask questions.

2. Independent reading increases both vocabulary and reading fluency.

3. Reading at home can be a powerful supplement to classwork. Parents can encourage leisure reading by giving books or magazines as presents.

4. A good foundation in speaking and listening helps children become better readers.

5. Learning to count everyday objects is an effective basis for early arithmetic lessons.

6. Although students need to learn how to find exact answers to arithmetic problems, good mathematics students also learn the helpful skill of estimating answers.

7. Accomplishment in a particular activity is often more dependent on hard work and self discipline than on innate ability.

8. Belief in the value of hard work, the importance of personal responsibility and importance of education contribute to greater success in school.

9. Parental involvement helps children learn faster and more effectively.

10. Children learn Science best when they are able to experiment, so they can witness "Science in action".

11. Parents (Teachers) who set and communicate high expectations to their children obtain greater academic performance from those who set low expectations.

12. How much time children are actively engaged in learning contributes strongly to their achievements.

13. Students tutoring other students can lead to improved academic achievement for both the student and the tutor, and to positive attitude towards coursework.

14. Memorising can help students absorb and retain the factual information on which understanding and critical thoughts are based.

15. Student's achievement rises when parents and teachers ask questions that require students to apply, analyse, synthesise and evaluate information in addition to simply recalling facts.

16. Students' achievement rises significantly when they conscientiously do their homework set by the teachers.

Case Studies

1. Joyful Memories of Parenting: As a parent I have often visualised (myself) as a tight-rope walker who walks on the rope with a balancing bar in her hands. On one end of the bar is stern discipline and on the other is unconditional love. A perfect balance between the two is effective parenting.

It is not quite as simple as that because you have to add to this the third factor which takes into account the unique personality of the child. Some children need more of discipline and others more of love.

The eldest child often teaches the parents the art of parenting, for they themselves are novices at it till then. With my first child I had the zeal to do everything right and the bar was tilted towards stern discipline. I retrospectively feel that I missed out on listening to my child's viewpoint or desires. I have since had to make ample amends for that. So I did achieve the stern discipline but at a cost. With the second child it was less discipline and more of love. As a result, the confidence level of the child was certainly higher but the discipline was lacking. I had swayed my bar to the other end. There is no third chance to show the right balance now!

Infancy is easier to handle but as adolescence or teenage approaches, the going gets tough. The two important areas to keep tabs on are pocket money and their interest in their core curriculum. At this age, the distractions are many...

As regards pocket money, I was lucky. Both my children were sensible spenders and I realised that I could maintain a very flexible attitude of allowing them of choosing the allowance they desired for that month. This, we maintained till they graduated from school and college. This may not work for all children but I do feel that taking the child's input while deciding their pocket money leaves them with less grudges.

Sharing your child's study time helps to maintain his/her interest in studies. If you sit with your child while they study even when they are studying in higher classes or subjects that you do not comprehend, your mere presence is helpful. I have often sat with my own reading while my children prepared for exams. This way they could break the monotony by talking to me and I could make them a drink or a snack if it got boring. You could even pursue one of your hobbies at this time for which you get so little time during the working day.

To sum up, there are only two tips that you have to adhere to very firmly during parenting. One is dead honesty in your interactions with your children. This is the strongest pillar of your relationship. It is only by showing honesty yourself that you can expect it in return. Do not be afraid of the embarrassment that honesty can sometimes cause; believe me, in the long run it will all iron out. Admitting your shortcomings only increases your respect. Seeing you trying to overcome your shortcomings is a great way of teaching your youngsters.

The second, and slightly harder to do at times, is to unwind the clock and put yourself in your child's shoes, to be able to understand his/her perspective. Then his fears appear genuine and his emotions are understandable.

I must confess here that parenting offers you the best chance of evolving your own personality. The ennobling qualities of love, compassion and sacrifice are only learnt through effective parenting. In other words, it is effective parenting that makes you a channel via which these divine qualities flow from the Almighty to your progeny, enriching their lives.

Dr. Mala Arora

FRCOG (UK), DA (UK), D'Obst (IRE), FICMCH (India)

Consultant Obstetrician & Gynaecologist

Sector 14, Faridabad

2. Even as I pen down my thoughts, I am indeed proud to say, that we, my better half and me, have had the good fortune of not merely bringing into the world, three lovely creations of God, but also nurturing them with love and care, like a gardener would a well-tended patch of land, and watching them blossom into young adults with now children of their own.

The path of parenthood that we trod upon, has been a roller-coaster ride, complete with its shares of ups and downs, high and low. A thrilling yet content journey filled with both sweet and salty (but not bitter) memories, though not ones my wife or I would have liked to be different or traded for anything in the world. As we travel down the memory lane, we both distinctly remember the birth of our three children Poonam, Deepak and Jyoti Despite being a traditional father in many respects, I have always tried to inculcate the basic values in my trio, whether they be moral, social, emotional or having a continual zeal and zest for life. Through our upbringing, we, as parents, have tried to achieve the rather difficult blend and balance of traditional with modernity. We have firmly believed in the adage that **while judging others, use your heart, but when judging yourself, use your mind.** We hope that, as parents, we have got the message that it is most important for an individual to try and succeed in every aspect of life while retaining certain values and certainly not at, the cost of others, firmly ingrained in our children's minds. A positive attitude, the drive to excel, balanced living, forward planning, no procrastinating or complacency, spiritualism, compassion for your friends, a close-knit family, working hard and playing hard are the important points to be taken care of when practising what you preach to your children. It is most important for a parent to always 'be there' for the children, a role which my wife Mrs. Narula aptly played to the hilt. She has always been there for the children, be it when taking them to religious places, theatres, the park or in helping them do their work. In fact, in this respect, she has always 'been there', even for me, her husband, and my success and subsequently our children's success in life can largely be attributed to her abilities to tackle diversity with a balance that is noteworthy. Though the intent was never to make them dependant, as an indulgent father, I have always tried my best to give my children that extra start which I hope has led them to traverse that extra mile with ease. Right through their schooling and college, both my wife and I have tried to present the right opportunities to our children, without succumbing to the easy way out. As a result, we are proud to reflect that our children did considerably well in their schooling years both academically and in co-curricular activities, be it games, debates, dramatics, shouldering responsibilities in the school or contributing to the school magazine. I must mention here that our children were lucky that the values instilled by us were reinforced by the school under the guidance of the then Principal Mr. S.C. Arora.

Our daughter Poonam is an M.B.A. from I.I.M. Bangalore, and well-settled in life, aiming higher with each passing day. After having resigned from ABN-Amro Bank, she has started her own Senior Secondary School (Dubai International Academy) in Meadows, Dubai. Our sons Deepak and Jyoti, have done their Ph.D. from Columbia University and M.B.A. from the University of Massachusetts respectively and still doing us proud. Deepak was earlier Senior Vice-President with Lehman Brothers at Wall Street but now he successfully runs his own Meta Capital Finance Company while Jyoti is the Managing Director of Genesis Colors (P) Ltd. and the joint owner of Satya Paul.

In the end, we would like to conclude by saying that the road, we, as parents have travelled, has been challenging and tough but one on which we wish we could re-trace our steps to re-live the joyous and pleasurable moments that only parenthood can bring. I would like to mention here a wise quote which goes, "A hundred years later, it may not matter which house I lived in or the fancy car that I drove, **but the world may be a better place to live in, because I was important in the life of a child.**" My sincere advice to all you aspiring parents is, **be that important factor in the life of your child and those around you.**

A.M. Narula

Postmaster General (Retd.) Vasant Vihar, New Delhi

———————————✳———————————✳———————————

3. As parents, at times, we tend to stray away from our priorities in life among which one of the most important is our responsibility towards our children. Our unintentional neglect starts to build up within them *lava* which can end up in a volcanic eruption at a particular point in their life. To avoid this from happening we should spend quality time with our children, assure them from time to time that we have confidence in them and give them freedom along with regular guidance.

Now, Karan is twelve-year old boy, almost ready to enter his teens. Going down memory lane, I remember I started reading to him very early, I used to get him more books than toys. He used to play with books also at times. He developed such a craze for stories that he would not go to bed until I read to him. He would listen very carefully and ask many questions when I read. This habit helped in arousing his curiosity. When he was around eight-year-old he started reading out stories to me which helped him in honing his reading skills. It used to give me such immense pleasure to see him sitting surrounded with books and deeply engrossed in them, which just goes to prove that the patience I had put in bore such sweet fruit. "Not all the world's treasure and gold can match the mother who had stories told." That's the best gift you can give your children.

I've always tried not to use in front of him the type of language I would not want him to use. We try never to criticise or discuss any bad habits of close friends or relatives in front of him. There's ample time to talk when the child is not around. Yes, but whenever necessary we do remind him of certain people's habits which he should be aware of and guide him how to deal with them. It has been made very clear to him that he must always respect his elders.

From time to time both of us keep giving him examples of friends who try to mislead him into wrong habits like drinking, smoking, drugs etc. which is a big nuisance today. Talking to children about these things and guiding them in a friendly manner can, to a great extent, help to keep them away from wrong company and acts.

Another thing I strongly feel about is that we should never indulge in criticising our children's teachers. Criticising in no way is the solution to any problem. It's just an easy way to put things on others' shoulders. However, in case a teacher is not up to the mark, we must try and sort out things by going to the child's school. Never forget that the responsibility of your child does not lie on the teacher and the school alone. You too are equally responsible.

As far as academics is concerned, Karan had always been doing very well from the beginning. But once a child gets good grades, the expectations of parents also rise. But we must remember that one or two per cent up or down does not make any difference at all. Putting pressure on the child has an adverse effect. Once a child is around eight to ten year old, depending upon your child, he should be given the independence to work on his own with of course your guidance whenever he requires it. This builds up the child's confidence and makes him more responsible. The more we spoon-feed him the more dependent he will remain on us. (This is from personal experience).

I always make it a point to teach him Nature ethics from time to time by telling him that nature is very precious. We must take care not to hurt it. We live if plants and animals live. I keep reminding him to switch off the lights whenever not required, not to waste paper by using old copies as rough copies, to keep our home and surroundings clean and specially not to waste water as it is very precious and there is always a shortage. None of these requires much effort and now these duties have become a habit.

The key to kill examination fear is regular studies. I make sure that my child allocates at least two hours of study for his homework and revision daily. That way he is regularly in touch with the topics done in class. Another thing a child should take care of is that all his homework and class work is completed on time and checked by the teacher. If that's done half the job is done. Writing works miracles for learning anything the child finds difficult to memorise. At least a week before the exams he has done one revision of all the subjects. Never leave any lesson untouched for one day before the exams. That increases anxiety and fear in the child's mind. During his exams I make sure to tell him that I'm around and that he can take my help whenever he requires.

As far as pocket-money is concerned, I give him around Rs. 200/- a week which takes care of his canteen expenses or a pencil he wants to buy in the school. Other than that we go shopping together and his requirements such as games, shoes, clothes, gifts for friends' birthdays etc. are met. I remind him from time to time that he should take care of his belongings and be grateful for what he has and must learn to respect it. Any carelessness from his side could get him into trouble for his future demands. A little firmness teaches them to value things. Getting things easily does not give us the right to become careless.

Mrs. Sureena Uppal

Panchsheel Enclave, New Delhi

4. It's not easy being a parent, sometimes you feel more like being a referee than a father or mother, but that goes with the territory. There are a few simple guidelines that I have tried to follow to keep good harmony in the home, for example to set reasonable expectations and goals for the family. I don't expect my children to come home with straight As and excel in academic and co-curricular activities. But, I do expect the children to at least do their best, whether at work, rest or play and that the children should know that they have put in their best effort, whether a school assignment, football practice or laying the table.

I believe that children flourish with firm guidance, they should know and feel confident within set boundaries. An example would be a good routine for small children, meals and naps at set times and bedtimes too. The day could be rounded off with a bedtime story, a signal that it is time to calm down and sleep, not to be leaping around and playing games. Be reasonable, gentle and firm.

Respect your children and yourself, prevent and minimise misunderstandings through good communication. Keep talking and be inclusive, otherwise children will seek attention elsewhere. Mealtimes are always a good time to unwind and find out what occurred during the school day. Anecdotes both from parents and children of the day's happenings provide reinforcement and encourage children to think and make choices. Include children into the dilemmas faced in the adult world. There is good value education provided covertly at the meal table.

I have always had faith in my children's abilities and never underestimated them. I trust that they can go out and play in the park or even go to the local shop without adult supervision. The rule set in stone being 'play safe, be safe'. I have never minced words and told the facts whether discussing 'stranger danger' or traffic rules.

Like it or loathe it, homework is a part of your child's school life and therefore a part of yours. For very young children, parents should be involved, a more hand on approach is required and praise given for all the child's efforts. For older children, parents should hover around and give encouragement but children should do their own work so that the concepts are clear.

As exams loom large on the horizon, help your child to prepare a study timetable and make sure that your child understands what is to be learnt, all goals and targets are clear. Younger children obviously welcome interaction and help in learning concepts. Older children should be able to revise on their own but again create an atmosphere so that your child knows that you are concerned and able to give guidance at any time. Make examination time stress free. Children should know that they are valued member of the family whether an A+ or a D result finally appears. I have always enjoyed reading and wanted the same for my children. I read to my children well before their first birthday and the reading habit stuck, now they read on their own. Reading a bedtime story or spending twenty minutes together pouring over a good book is well worthwhile. Children learn a great deal, imaginative stories, interesting use of the language and in addition a strong bond is developed between parent and child. I have enjoyed revisiting my favourite childhood authors, recommending and reading them to my own children.

Make a point to spend some part of the day with your children, whether it is over breakfast, catching some time between homework, at dinner or at bedtime. Make sure the moment is relaxed (play a game like Snakes and Ladders, cards etc.) and find out what is happening in your child's life. You should be able to spend undivided time together and pay attention! If you are too busy, make it clear that you will be free at a certain time later on and stick to that agreement.

Children mirror their parents. Values are first taught within the confines of the home and family followed by school and peer group. As a parent, it is important to treat all people with civility, courtesy and dignity, be honest, trustworthy and respectful, show courage and diligence. Your children are watching you. Your children are searching around and trying to construct a vision of themselves, help them live up to that vision. You can show them that in a world where poor character is commonplace, they can choose to be better than that.

Mrs. Helen Kant

Sector 29, Faridabad

5. Talking through experience, brought up two children - a girl and a boy, I can very confidently say that parenting is a very exciting and satisfying experience.

The secret of my parenting has been open communication with my children at every stage of their growth process—childhood, adolescence and adulthood. I took special care to ensure that they shared their feelings, opinions and observations with me without any inhibition or a sense of fear/scare.

Although it was often me who had to take that one step extra to initiate the dialogue whenever we all were in a conflicting situation, it eased the stress levels and helped in resolving the problem. A warm hug after the dialogue always brought a smile on everyone's face. But there is no denying the fact that it demanded a reasonable amount of patience, compassion and understanding.

Like all growing children they too committed their own mistakes. However, I was conscious enough not to overreact and outrightly condemn their behaviour. I attempted to handle the situation delicately.

I have enjoyed being a friend to them. I always understood their point of view and gave my inputs more as a friend than just a parent who would put across only her own do's and don'ts. At the same time I never forgot to be firm when required even if it led to momentary unpleasantness.

I also made it a point to see that they were not put under any undue pressure that normally evolves due to the hidden desires of parents wanting their children to excel as per their predetermined standards. It is so important to rationalise the capabilities of your child and give them a direction accordingly.

My efforts were also to make them see the positive aspects of life rather than focusing on the negativities. This approach, I feel has helped them to grow up with a cheer and a smile on their faces. Reflecting now, I feel that, having pursued a balanced approach in the process of parenting led them to discover the path of their choice.

What better compliment can one expect when your own child expresses the desire to be able to bring up her children with a similar approach to parenting.

Anita Paul

Principal

Apeejay School, Saket, New Delhi

6. When we recently visited our daughter, Shagufa, in Australia, we were pleased to see her in the role of a loving wife, a caring mother and an efficient executive all rolled into one. We would look at each other with a smile whenever we saw her reprimanding her elder daughter on wasting anything because it reminded us of her unmarried days when she won't care about things.

Shagufa was a spendthrift and would not put much value on money as it came easily. We made her the Principal of Flowrence Public School which we were ourselves running and fixed her salary at Rs. 5,000/- p.m. hoping she would learn to use money properly but no, she would be out the whole day after receiving her salary and come back in the evening declaring "finished" as if a very big burden had been lifted of her shoulders. She would finish the salary feeding the poor, serving ice-cream to street dogs! and some shopping. Feeding the poor was understandable but treating the dogs with ice-cream was unheard of. She would explain that they don't get to taste ice-cream at all, hence her generosity.

She had to be taught the value money and we were looking for an opportunity. One day on a family outing she expressed her desire to buy gold bangles which she had liked immensely. Both of us seized the opportunity and told her that if she contributed half the amount the remaining half would be put by her father. As a result Shagufa started saving for the bangles. The purpose was achieved by tactful handling rather than scolding, shouting or ordering. We were happy to note that she, a mother of two children now, imbibed the values we were wanting to instil.

Another incident where we achieved the desired result was with our son, Sumant. I took out some time from my extremely busy schedule to witness a football match my 8 years old son was participating in.

When finally the teams had lined up it took me considerable time to locate my little one as he was the youngest and the shortest in both the teams. I was a little anxious about Sumant's well-being and wondered whether he will be able to play with those burly boys. Throughout the game my Chotu' ran and ran and ran all over the field but got no chance to be near the ball, leave aside kick it. All this time I was cheering him loudly, endlessly hoping and praying to God to give him a chance to prove his mettle: but to no avail. As luck would have it Sumant's team won. My sweaty, dishevelled, excited Sumant came running to me after the game and anxiously asked me how he had done. I didn't know how to react and just burst out crying, but instantly controlled myself, embraced him, patted him and told him how well he had played. On his enquiry I told him that the tears were of happiness and pride. Next day with pride in his eyes Sumant brought home the gold medal he had received as a member of the winning team. I hugged him tight and proudly showed it around to everyone.

Sumant is now a grown up man with children, running his software company successfully both is U.S.A. and India. It was my encouragement and faith in him that kept up his enthusiasm in life where he is a 'winner'. The same medal is one of my coveted possessions and still adorns the mantleshelf at our house.

Mrs. Meena Ahuja

Sector 17, Noida

7. I am Asha Chhikara, mother of three kids two daughters and a son, of ages 17, 19 and 23 now.

My vision in bringing them up was to be able to give first-rate education in order to see them as accomplished personalities. Two of them are taking education from world-renowned prestigious institutes. And have built recognitions of their own by bringing laurels to their institutes in different ways.

At present my two daughters are at the University in America and my son is now a graduate. Achieving success in raising them as high character individuals, while bringing them up, has not been easy and required tremendous patience. The following quote learnt from my father "if wealth is lost nothing is lost, health is lost something is lost and if character is lost then everything is lost" has' been my source of inspiration.

In order to provide good parenting I pursued the following steps in general.

One of the most important points I always kept in mind was to avoid any arguments between my husband and myself in the presence of my children.

Secondly in order to maintain each child's self-esteem and confidence I never let any child down in front of other siblings. Keeping my cool, I waited for the right time to have interaction individually.

Thirdly, was to engage in maximum dialogue with my children on any and every topic related to their age concerns and develop a bond where they could trust me with all their thoughts.

While giving them exposure to almost all things I never compromised on educating them about value of money. Though my children studied in boarding schools in latter years of their schooling, I visited them at least once a month, if needed twice. Seeking advice from school teachers by attending all parent-teacher meetings has been a regular practice. In addition to all these facts, I never stopped searching and practising together with them, spiritualism that could empower me to groom my children even better. Finally, in 1996 I encountered Nichiren Daishonin's Buddhism, a life philosophy, whose basic teaching is to respect all human beings and this value I have inculcated in my children by encouraging them to join me in the Buddhist practise.

Asha Chikara

Malviya Nagar, New Delhi

8. We feel very privileged to write this article on our experience in parenting our wonderful sons. It gives us immense pleasure that you thought of us for this write up.

To be honest with you, we have not given a serious thought about how good our parenting skills were. We cannot make tall claims. However, on reflecting back, I think we had been parents with deep commitment towards our children. Our priority in life has always been the future of our sons. We were very close to them. Our life has been an open book to them. They have observed how we embraced achievements, failures, struggles and challenges. Probably this transparency has helped them to accept us as we are with our strengths as well as vulnerabilities. This might have helped them in self acceptance as well. They were not ashamed of faltering and learning from bad experiences. We have always appreciated how hard our sons worked in every endeavour irrespective of whether they succeeded or not. We have resisted the temptation to compare them with any other person. We are grateful that they are not comparing us with other wonderful parents.

We have free and open communication with our children. We not only love them but, respect them as well. From childhood they felt free to question us anything that bothered them. We explained things in age-appropriate levels. We apologized when we were wrong. We tried our best to practise what we preached. We tried to teach them by our own example that to be obedient to elders & teachers is a mark of good grooming and not meekness.

It was indeed a big challenge to deal with the financial constraints of a middle-class family. We sacrificed our personal wants and provided their educational needs. When our children were young, they wanted to celebrate their birthdays with pomp and show like their wealthy friends. We are happy that we had the serenity and patience to explain them how important it is to live within one's means. To our surprise the little ones understood the value of money and frugality as a value.

Our children learnt to appreciate worthy opponents who won them in competitions. They realized that they have to grow taller and not to cut others short. Regarding academics we monitored their class work and homework regularly. We allowed them to do the homework themselves & offered help only when they needed. Though it is time consuming and demands immense patience to supervise, it is worth it inculcating self-learning. We helped them to have a regular study—play—recreation schedule. We trained them to use time carefully and fruitfully, calculate approximately the time needed for completing tasks, fix target date and organise work. We avoided social life which disturbed children's study and sleep schedule.

'Children adore their parents when they are young.

They understand them as they grow.

They forgive them as they mature.'

We have had our own share of bad parenting. We realise that we had been too protective. We never let our sons go for adventure trips or choose paths less travelled in life. Our children do not blame us for this. They are venturing all these unfulfilled desires now.

If our sons are brilliant academicians and good human beings, it is the grace of God and the motivation provided by great teachers like Mr. Arora. We cannot forget how his guidance and encouragement ignited the spark of enthusiasm in my son Kamal Nayan and brought out his best potentials. The caring and reassuring counselling of Madam Arora helped my son Anand Nayan to emerge as a scholar and responsible prefect. We are indebted to you both & their teachers.

Nirmala Jayaraman and V Jayaraman

P.S.: Kamalnayan Jayaraman graduated from University of Delhi in Electronics and Communication Engineering. He was awarded the Chief Minister's Gold Medal for his outstanding performance and for being the University Topper.

He did his Masters in Electrical and Computer Engineering from University of Texas, Austin, USA. He is presently working with Intel Corporation, Chandler, Arizona, USA as CAD engineer in the test technology group.

Anandnayan Jayaraman graduated from Anna University, Chennai, Tamilnadu in Instrumentation Technology. He was awarded Gold Medal for standing first in the University. He is currently pursuing his Masters from University of Wisconsin, Madison, USA.

Now to put into effect all the suggestions which I

have given is the province of prayer, perhaps of

exhortation. And even to follow zealously

the majority of them demands, good fortune and

much careful attention, but to accomplish this

lies within the capability of man.

- Plutarch, 46-120 A.D.

Tips for Ready Reference

1. **Be understanding and supportive of your child:** Growing up children are, at times, bound to act silly, misbehave, be rude, embarrass you etc. Be understanding of your children as most of us have indulged in this type to behaviour during our early life. Instead of punishing or reprimanding instantly, find the cause of their misdemeanour, then counsel them; explain to them the consequences of their disturbing action. It is only by being supportive that their behaviour can be modified.

2. **Satisfy and arouse their curiosity:** Children are curious by nature, about various things. That is how they make sense of the world. Actually, curiosity is fundamental to learning. If we keep quenching and arousing their curiosity the children are bound to gain knowledge. It will become a habit with them and then there will be no stopping in life.

3. **Trust your child but verify:** The more we trust our children, the more they will become trustworthy. Since trust begets trust, they will begin to believe you too. But on many occasions, I have seen children giving false excuses for not having done homework or absenting themselves from school. At times, they have gone to the

extent of signing their own answer sheets and the Report Cards on behalf of their parents. Mostly things are okay, but in a few cases where children have indulged in undesirable acts, it becomes necessary to keep one's eyes open.

4. **Be honest in your dealings with the school:** It is desirable that the school and the parents should be on the same page, at all times. Therefore, do not make false excuses on behalf of your child. If your child has not done the homework because he was lazy, do not put up an excuse for him. The truth be mentioned to the school for bringing attitudinal change in the child.

5. **Let the child follow his dreams:** You cannot help passing on your genes to your child but do not see the child as *your extension.* Let him not realise *'your'* dreams. If the child is not good at math but is excellent in fine arts, let him pursue that. Allow him to dream big and realise "his" dreams. Who knows he may be the next Satish Gujral or Amitabh Bachchan, Sania Mirza, Bill Gates or Binny Bansal (co-founder, Flipkart).

6. **Make your child a thinker:** There are numerous opportunities of learning in life. Suppose you and your child have just finished watching a cartoon strip. Most people will ask the child whether he liked it or not. After the child has given the answer 'yes' or 'no', parents miss an excellent chance of making the child think. The next natural question would be, why he did or did not like? It is at this stage that the thinking process begins. Parents must utilise this technique of making the children put their thinking caps on. They must continue to ask children age_appropriate, searching, thought-provoking questions. 'How, why, when, where, what, who, whose' are the best teachers in life!

7. **Encourage critical thinking:** Exchange ideas with your kids. Discuss the pros and cons of those ideas. Give them an opportunity to defend their ideas. Allow them to

criticize your ideas. Let them look for various possible alternatives to solving a particular problem. This kind of churning of their minds gives the youngsters an opportunity to think in divergent ways and introduces fluency and clarity in their ability to think.

8. **Help your child to go beyond critical thinking:** For critical thinking, you need a problem to be critical about. Suppose you have severe headache. You will immediately go to the doctor. But one could avoid this by pro-active thinking *i.e.,* even if I have no symptoms of headache or high blood pressure or diabetes I could embrace the lifelong habits of healthy eating and regular exercise. Perhaps, I wouldn't develop any disease. Therefore, help your child anticipate future problems and take action to obviate those obstacles. Reassure him about his thinking and let him express and act on it.

9. **Provide a stimulating environment:** It depends upon your ability as a parent: how much your child explores from a toy car or Lego building blocks or even from home utility items in a creative fashion. Through these materials the child is not only able to make productive use of his free time but also can explore novel ideas. The parent can further identify from the innovative expression of the child the bent of his mind and provide further support.

10. **Keep encouraging the child:** Just recall a situation at your workplace when you presented a novel idea in your board meeting and instead of criticizing you, the management listened to you with immense patience. The amount of confidence and the joyous feeling you felt was unfathomable. The same is the situation with children. Do not condemn them for kiddish or unachievable ideas. No novel ideas are silly. Archimedes, Wright Brothers, Vijay Shekhar Sharma (founder, Paytm), Sachin Bansal (co-founder, Flipkart), Steve Jobs, Elon Musk, with all of them, in the beginning their ideas appeared silly and unachievable.

11. **Let children be not deterred by failure:** Let the child learn by doing. He may fail to achieve the target a couple of times. But keep encouraging and he will succeed. The bend in the road is not the end of the road. It may just be a road-bump. Failure is natural in life. Encourage him to develop a positive outlook in life. "Let him see the silver lining in the dark cloud" (William Blake). All life-fulfilling experiences arise from a positive state of mind. You may mention to the child your own few failures where you finally succeeded. Laugh off his failures and affirm his success. Failure followed by success gives immense boost to child's self-confidence.

    Failures we suffer at the hands of others are nothing: they can be easily handled. What is scary is failures we experience inside us. That is what we have to guard against. Therefore, let us ingrain in our children that they have not failed till they stop trying. It they continue to persevere, they are bound to succeed.

12. **Teach the kids to work for self-fulfillment:** At young age, rewards may be required but finally everybody must work for self-fulfillment. Let children not excel in some task merely for a gold medal or having an Ivy League degree on their C.V. but for their own growth, mental satisfaction and happiness. This will ensure smooth navigation throughout their lives.

13. **Encourage him to take responsibility:** There may be situations when your child comes back home from school or from the playground troubled and in tears as a result of having fought with a fellow mate. This is the time to teach him to take on the responsibility of resolving his conflicts on his own. He should, of course be sure that help would be forthcoming, in case of need. Every situation can be an opportunity for learning some trait of life.

14. **Health is Wealth:** फिट रहेंगे, तो हिट रहेंगे

    It is a truism that a healthy mind can reside only in a healthy body. Unfortunately, a remote controlled style of living has reduced in physical effort. This has led to a sedentary life for all age groups. In all major towns of the country, increasingly we find the children are getting flabby, almost obese, and hence falling prey to all kinds of diseases. Therefore, it is absolutely necessary that children of all ages be sensitized to the need for physical fitness. It is my belief that those, irrespective of age, who cannot find time to take some kind of exercise will have to find time to visit the doctor not once but many times. It is well known that prevention is better than cure and, therefore, everybody must make an effort to keep himself physically fit, reducing the possibility of falling ill.

Growing up children need nutritious diet for a healthy body. So, kindly ensure that your child's diet includes the necessary nutrients i.e., carbohydrates, proteins, vitamins, healthy fats and roughage, iron and other minerals. In addition, plenty of exercise is needed for remaining healthy.

Swami Vivekananda exhorted the youth, *"Be strong, my young friends....You will be nearer to heaven through football than through the study of the Gita....you will understand the Gita better with your biceps, your muscles a little stronger. You will understand the mighty genius and the mighty strength of Krishna better with a little of strong blood in you. You will understand the Upanishads better and the glory of the Atma when your body stands firm on your feet..."*

15. **Raise the confidence level of the child.** If your child possesses self-confidence, he can achieve anything in life. Therefore, help your child to build a positive self-image; he should see himself as worthy, able and good. To achieve this, keep giving positive strokes like 'well done', 'star performance', 'wow, you played the guitar very well'. Appreciate him often, do not condemn. Affirmative words boost the self-esteem of the child.

Celebrate small wins and achievements of your child. Build on their strengths, catch them doing right, "you made your bed without being asked—that's terrific". Don't compare with peers or siblings. Unfavourable comparison with another child will make him feel worthless. Instead, encourage your child to benchmark against himself. Encourage your child to pursue some activity which interests him. Proficiency in a hobby will boost his morale. Have intimate interaction with him for stronger emotional bond.

It is important for you to be aware that negative comments would wound the child; genuine praise will empower him.

16. **Goal Setting**: "Alice: Would you tell me please, which way I ought to go from here?

    Cat: That depends a good deal on where you want to get.

    Alice: I don't much care where.

    Cat: If you don't know where you are going, any road will take there."

    Lewis Caroll, Alice in Wonderland.

    It is absolutely necessary to help the child in setting up an age-appropriate goal. If there is no goal, he will just drift. The goal could be as trivial as retrieving a thing from a difficult position, kicking a ball up to a distance of 30 meters, scoring half a century or do six lengths of the swimming pool. For teenagers, the target could be to reach 85% from 80% or learning to bowl a googly or a Yorker. Seniors could dream of scoring 100% in maths or as a long term goal, become an entrepreneur or a space scientist or the chief justice of India. This help has to be provided to children not by a direct sermon but through a casual conversation or by giving examples of young achievers. We have to further caution children that there will be mistakes and missteps in actualizing their vision but that is natural. We have to further assist children in building up determination to see things through. We should keep constantly **raising their self-belief.**

Believing firmly that something can be done unleashes not only immense inner forces but even the cosmic powers synergize to find a way to do it. So let children not be limited in their perception. Let them dream big and believe that they can realize the same. Beliefs of human beings are their psychological bandwidths. Let us help children in expanding their bandwidths.

17. **Life skills:** We are living in the 21st century when unlike in the past no person will stick to one job. Whatever one learns at school and college becomes obsolete within a few months. And hence, such knowledge will not be of much help to the child in later life. What will be of use are life skills. Therefore, our endeavour as parents would be to support the child in developing life skills like effective communication, intent listening, self-restraint, alertness, teamwork, empathy, harmony with nature, anger management, time management, decision making etc. **These personality traits will prove more useful than an academic gold medal.** The training in these characteristics will lead him to achieve success. With my experience with thousands of children, I have come to the conclusion that one may get A^+ grade and yet flunk in life without the above mentioned life skills.

18. **Value system:** Values are those intangible rules by which individuals make decisions about what ought to be done or avoided. They are *just* behaviours in action. They are caught rather than taught. Children observe and imitate the significant adults in their lives. Therefore, parents need to practice the values they espouse. If children observe their parents telling lies, receiving or giving bribes, being rude, lazy or eating junk food, they will begin to think that this is acceptable behaviour and will internalize the same value system. Hence, parents ought to model the traits they wish their children to emulate. Good values can also be instilled by narrating

episodes and stories culled from history and religious scriptures. Parables woven around values is another source.

Parents should be careful about what books children read or watch cartoon strips or what kind of movies they watch. Any material propagating violence, foul or abusive langauge or discriminating between caste, creed or religion, race or colour of skin must be carefully avoided. It is extremely important, more so these days, to sensitize them about gender, race or colour of the skin bias. Train them to respect women and people of the whole world. A strong culture be created at home that to uphold moral and human values becomes second nature to children.

19. **Pursuit of excellence**: Let us recall a few lines from Richard Bach's Jonathan Livingston Seagull.

Jonathan: Is there no such place as heaven?

Chiang: No, Jonathan there is no such place. Heaven is not a place, and it is not a time. Heaven is pursuit of excellence. Excellence does not have any limits.

Excellence does not come to a person who sits in hope with arms folded; **it is granted to a man who rolls up his sleeves and labours.** Excellence is an individual quest whereas mediocrity is a collective refuge. Parents would do well to be conscious to ingrain in their children the **passion for excellence.** Keep pointing out to them that anything which is worth doing is worth doing very well. Otherwise, one doesn't enjoy. We shall have to keep guiding our progeny, that for pursuit of excellence, they will have to develop a sharp unrelenting focus, if required to the exclusion of all else. All achievers do that. Film-stars, sports icons, writers, musicians, artists, athletes, researchers, scholars—every discipline demands focused dedication.

Portuguese Cristiano Ronaldo, footballer par excellence, says he is relentless in his pursuit of excellence "to live the dream that he never wants to wake up from"

Direct sermons to children or making authoritative statements, without explanations, do not work. The guidance, the advice has to be woven into a casual talk, loosely packed. If all this is administered through sweetened pills, I can assure you, your child will shine in life.

The quality of a person's life is in direct proportion to his commitment to excellence regardless of his chosen field of endeavour.

20. **Keep the channels of communication open:** At the root of our humanness is connection. The need for intimate and meaningful relationship is present in our wiring at birth and through death. There will always be occasions when there will be disagreements, heated discussions and breaking of communication between you and your child. In such situations don't ever label the child as bad. Only a particular act of the child is not acceptable. But, the child still remains good. No purpose will be served by blaming, criticizing or fault finding. These hurt the self-esteem, leading to resentment and unnecessarily aggravating the situation. The child must understand that your love for him is unconditional.

    To be able to deal effectively with children you must be at peace with yourself. You have to resolve your own inner conflicts and be sure about your philosophy of parenting. Even when a tiff takes place don't ever break the channels of communication. Basically, children would like to keep their parents in good humour. Hence you must not have any ego issue with your child. Try to decode what is going on underneath it all. Your endeavour must be to listen to the child and resolve the issue. Be open to your child's suggestions as well. Be non-judgmental. Be a supportive listener by giving the child full attention. He will definitely respond.

Conclusion 

I have tried to give the parents the gist of what I have learnt about bringing up children. After reading what all I have said you may feel squeezed like a mop, thinking that parenting is a herculean task. But really speaking it need not be so: if you love your children unconditionally (which you do) and are motivated enough to see their balanced growth and are aware of what's happening to them, you will enjoy every moment of their lives. There are no hard and fast rules nor does any manual give instructions to deal with the plethora of knotty situations which arise as we are rearing children. This work cannot be outsourced to the school. You have to bring them up yourself and it is the most important work you do in the world. Parenthood is the most important leadership responsibility in life.

Parenting is necessarily a balancing act. It's like flying a kite, sometimes you loosen the string and other times you tighten it for the kite to go up. At times, you have to give in and other times, **you have to be firm and ready to say 'no' to your child.** To make children responsible you should not do things for them that they are capable of doing themselves. By encouraging them to take care of themselves you will foster a sense of self-sufficiency and competency. Remember, the child has his own individual strengths and weaknesses with a flavour of his own identity. Therefore, **no effort should be made to mould the child in your** image: **respect his/her uniqueness.** You only need to provide an environment where the child can breathe air of freedom in order to grow. Since we are interested not only in widening the horizon of the child but his thinking capacity also, we should keep our eyes open to situations where they can look for patterns, common threads, how do things relate, how things happen — the reason behind the phenomenon (e.g. refraction causes rainbow). Challenge your kid with thoughts like what would happen if there was no sun? Or if all cars were painted black? Or if people wore the shirts of the same brand? A visit to the zoo or the museum should not be only confined to seeing things but we should give them information about animals and pieces of art or historical interest etc. Also we should **ask them questions which lead to thinking and arousal of curiosity.**

We should not worry unnecessarily when teenagers begin to form different opinions from that of ours or indulge in some dangerous activities or wear some odd clothes. They like to be different for getting attention or recognition: they will do anything to stand out ज़रा हटके *(Zara Hatke)*, boys wearing ear rings, girls getting their naval pierced. But this is a temporary phase and shall pass. I have seen all types of children, running noses in early childhood, shirts partly coming out of the trousers, torn shoes, shabby clothes, slovenly presented work, putting forward lame excuses for not doing homework, lazy in doing class work, long or short hair, skirts above or below the knees etc., growing up into well adjusted, respectable citizens of the world. Quite a few of my such students have become Chief Engineers, Scientists, Computer Programmers, Industrialists, Eminent Professors, Doctors, Bollywood Actors, T.V. stars, Vice Presidents and Presidents of various companies. The most important thing is that **we keep supervising, monitoring their attitudes and behaviour.** The key to success lies in **not giving up and remaining connected with them.** When differences arise, be available and remain engaged in the incidental and casual conversation: you will see that disagreements either vanish or in any case narrow. Don't let the gulf grow into canyon proportions. When in a particular situation the trust level is low, the matter may be referred to a third party (*Bhua, Masi, Chachi, Chacha, Mama,*

Mami, a family friend etc. whom the child likes) for arbitration: it helps. The self-respect of children should never be trampled upon. Bad Report-Card should never be discussed at the dining table. Reduce the time for viewing T.V. as it not only shortens the attention span, for no scene lasts for more than a couple of minutes, but also it is not nearly as mentally challenging as reading. In fact, it makes children passive recipients of soap operas of no real value at all.

Don't drink, don't speed etc. goes above the head of the child. Instead discussion of actual news items or articles where youngsters have harmed themselves by these acts will have better impact. When the child oversteps (and there are many such occasions) and you get agitated and the situation seems to be getting out of hand, don't press the panic button: use the technique, "I am upset now, I do not want to shout, we shall discuss it later". The trick is not to have a short fuse.

How poor are they that have no patience! What wound did ever heal but by degrees?

Shakespeare, Othello

My years in the teaching profession have taught me **that children are willing to change their behavioural patterns in return for love and recognition.** The reality is that they also like order in life: they do want adult guidance and **will accept it if it is appropriately and persuasively packaged.**

These are times of fast changes. New technologies are making old job skills obsolete. Therefore, the best preparation we can give our children is to make them alert, observant, help them in mastering the basic skills of Reading, Writing, Mathematics and Logical Reasoning, sense of Discipline and Hard Work. In addition, we can help them acquiring life skills like listening, communicating effectively, respecting elders, helping others, empathising, respecting others' point of view, stress management, emotion management, inter-personal skills, decision making, thinking for themselves and desire to learn: they enable individuals to deal effectively with life's diverse challenges.

Encourage the child to master a sport or a hobby: it helps not only to de-stress later when (s)he is grown up but also provides zest for life.

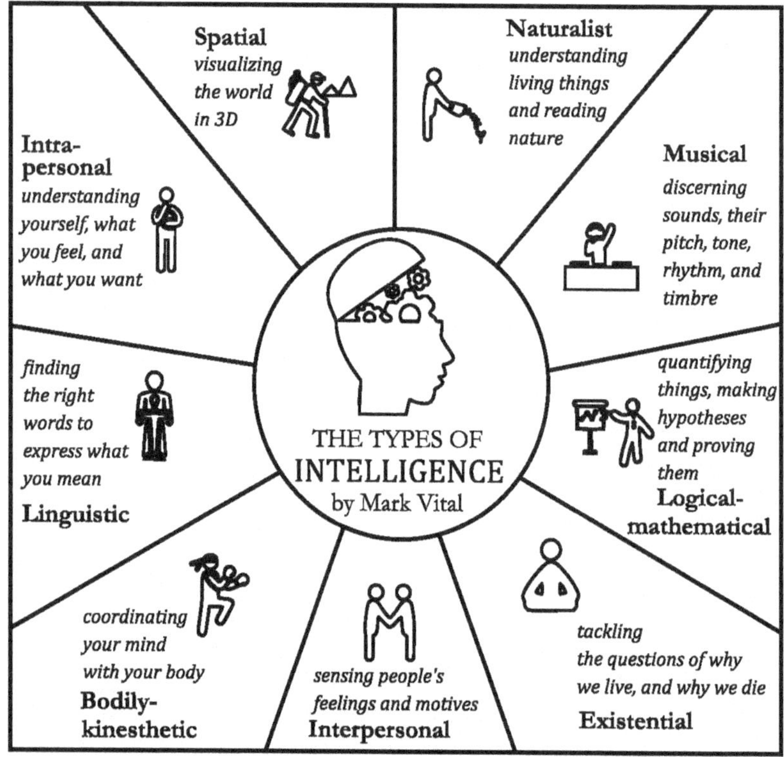

Nobody can excel at everything: Each child possesses a set of attributes and talents wherein he or she can perform admirably. If one child has an analytical mind, another may be manually dexterous and skillful; one may have an aptitude for fine arts and another may be endowed with musical talent. Who knows the academic marks of M.F. Hussain or Zakir Hussain of Taj fame or Lata Mangeshkar, but they have excelled in life. Your child is also bound to have some talent. Together you have to discover it and nurture it. If (s)he cannot be a Bill Gates, (s)he could be a Tendulkar or Manavjit Singh (Ace shooter) or Sania Mirza: If (s)he cannot be a Ravishankar, may be (s)he can emulate Narayanmurthy or Amitabh Bachchan. Howard Gardner has classified intelligence, in his theory of multiple intelligences and abilities, under nine heads, *viz* linguistic—verbal, logical—mathematical, visual—spatial, bodily, kinesthetic, musical—rhythmic, interpersonal, intrapersonal, naturalist and existentialist. You have to see which, out of these nine talents, your child possesses in abundance and then lead him/her onwards to shine in that field. Impress upon the child to pursue excellence rather than run after money. Lakshmi, Kuber or Mammon will automatically bless him/her. These characteristics are learnt more from the family than elsewhere. Recall the words of Indra Nooyi, the then C.E.O. of Pepsi Co., "My parents taught me that if you do a job, you must do it better than anybody else." Among other things human beings are primarily shaped by cultural and moral norms. And that is what parents ought to be doing, instilling a belief in the child in human goodness, their infinite potential and the conviction that they are capable of achieving any goal.

Avoid becoming a 'Helicopter' parent: Hovering over your child all the time and meddling in every area of his/her life, hampering his maturation, autonomy and future ability to cope with varied problems of the roller coaster life. Give him/her plenty of space to grow: let him play and explore without restraint. So long as he/she does not endanger his/her or others' life or remains away from harm's way let him continue to take minor decisions. But don't abdicate your responsibility as a parent. Remain the captain of the ship: the rudder should remain in your hands: the Remote control should remain in your possession to be operated when needed. **All this is possible to accomplish: we only need the will to do it.**

Don't underestimate your power to influence your child's behaviour. You can do a lot. You can enrich the development of your child in ways that classroom instructions can ever match. But, whether or not the child will receive your advice and guidance depends upon how you package it. Remember, it's a privilege of helping our children to discover and nurture their special gifts and talents. Don't feel overwhelmed by the complexity of the job. Although it is a daunting task to raise children of character, it is a very fulfilling job too. So long as you are loving, caring, dedicated, firm, a role model and invested in working hard, everything will work out well. The human frame carries a unique, huge reservoir of energy—beyond thought-mind level. Our aim as parents is to ignite the cosmic fire to release this energy. Your child is not born to crawl. He is destined to soar high. He is not meant to be a passenger; he has to be the pilot. He is a masterpiece in the making. Just be responsive, enabling parents. Don't outsource your job to service providers. Provide a loving, warm, intimate—sitting in a quilt type chat—environment. Have patience. Be assured, your child will be a great human being. He is bound to ace in life.

Centuries ago Socrates put to parents, "Why is it that you turn and scrape every stone to gather wealth and neglect your children to whom one day you must relinquish it all?"

It's one of those rare opportunities of a lifetime, to be invited by one's teacher, to write the epilogue for his book on Effective Parenting. This book is significant in many ways. It contains nuggets of experiences drawn from over five decades of engagement of Mr Arora with school education. It is also timely as its theme reflects one of the most serious challenges faced by today's generation of parents. Reading through its pages, I noticed that Mr Arora does not offer a prescriptive list of right and wrong but deals with the complex theme using the prism of approaches, attitudes and most critically acceptance.

As I read the fascinating range of anecdotes that Mr Arora presents, my mind goes back to 1974 – nearly four and a half decades ago. This was my first year of contact with Mr Arora, when he joined as the Principal of India School, Kabul, a school that I had joined a year earlier, in the 8th grade. As the Head Boy, I recall the dignity and grace with which Mr Arora greeted all the parents on different occasions that they participated in school functions. On one occasion, seeing my parents (with whom I was standing), he came up to them and complimented me for something (which I thought was quite routine) that had happened in the school in the previous week. I could see the pride in the eyes of my parents' and from that day on endeavoured to act in a manner that would keep that radiance on my parents face. Mr Arora's passion for excellence and capacity to "reach-out" was commendable. A few years ago, when I was sitting in his office prior to a function I had been invited for, a visitor jokingly asked him "Mr Arora, when will you retire?" In a moment came the response, "When did I start working to retire? It has been more than five decades of learning!"

One striking line in the book is Mr Arora's comment that there is "no problem child" and that "children never fail". What causes challenges is that they have not had the benefit of right mentoring. In this context he dwells on a few important themes. Firstly, he underscores the importance of creating the right environment for learning both at home and in the school, so that the children imbibe the values that allow them to make the right choices in life. Secondly, he highlights the importance of building a "culture of collaboration and cooperation" between the parents and the teachers. Thirdly, he focuses on the importance of the parents developing the right "listening skills" and dwells at length with the importance of parents spending time with their children. In my own teaching life, I remember a student who once asked his parents in my presence, "Can you spare half an hour a day to listen to me?" The parents were stunned and after a moment replied, "Son you need not ask for time, it is your right and we will make sure that we listen to what you have to say".

I also found the book, forcing the reader to sit back and reflect on what appears so simple, but could well be very complex. My wife Shailaja, a child psychologist, often says, "Talk to the child, Counsel the parents". Mr Arora draws attention to the dangers of "Dual Parenting", a situation that leaves the child confused and overtime learns to take advantage of. "Dual Parenting" often degenerates to "Duel Parenting"! The book makes out a strong case for the "power and influence of parenting" being the by-product of one experiencing the "Joys of Parenting". I am sure this book would help many parents understand the complexities of parenting and help them provide that environment which allows children to develop as wonderful human beings. Thank you Sir, for these gems of wisdom flowing from practical experience.

Dr. Sandeep Shastri

Pro Vice Chancellor

JAIN — a Deemed to be University

As I became a parent, I realized that bringing up my children was the most satisfying yet challenging experience I had ever been through. Arora sir was my Principal during my formative years in the school. His book "Effective Parenting" has come out as a boon for young parents who will get much desired guidance given by the author with his dozens of years of experience in dealing with children. He has suggested solutions to problems which confront the parents on daily basis. Mr. Arora believes that character traits and values along with indomitable spirit will enable the child to navigate the roller-coaster life with ease and confidence. Mr. Arora has suggested various activities to help parents to build up these attributes. I recommend this book to all young parents and grandparents who are in the process of raising kids.

Maniesh Paul

TV Host and Bollywood Actor

Principal Arora has written a wonderful book which is a guide for all parents today, especially young ones, on the challenges of raising their children. There can be no one better to write this, given Sir's extensive experience as an educationist. Having been his student, I would urge parents to read and learn from this book.

Nidhi Razdan

Executive Editor, NDTV

No operating manual accompanies the child at his birth. That is what Mr Arora's book does _ a manual to be followed by young parents with great benefit to their progeny. Mr Arora emphasizes on loving the child unconditionally irrespective of good or bad habits of children. He's of the opinion that if you catch your child doing the right things and affirm the same, the undesirable habits will fade away. He urges parents to create an atmosphere of learning whichever way they deem fit. Children learn more by emulating their parents than by their sermons. I am impressed by the brilliance and the positive attitude Mr Arora shows in his book, seasoned with practical anecdotes culled from his experience of life.

The author stresses upon giving sanskars and life-skills to the children so that they can lead an inspiring life. The book lays out a roadmap for parents for raising children. Mr Arora exhorts parents, that in addition to being a role model, they should treat their wards as unique individuals with characteristics embedded in their DNA.

RajatKhare

Founder, CMD, Boundary Holding (Luxemburg)

Motivational speaker & an author.

The author, Mr. S. C. Arora or Arora sir, as we fondly call him has been a constant source of inspiration. His parenting insights and advice have always helped me both in personal and professional life. His rich experience as a teacher, principal and mentor in the education fraternity is concentrated in the book as advice, guidance and inspiration; the more one reads this text, more comes to forth. The effectiveness of his techniques and ideas can be viewed in his students' lives today, several of whom are revered and distinguished personalities in the field of Education, Defense, Finance, Media and many others. However, true proof of the pudding is in eating. So I strongly recommend parents and educationists to go ahead and find answers to all your queries and anxieties. If successfully implemented, your child will become a winner in life and a great human being.

Poonam Yadav

Director, Little Pearls Group of Schools

This 112-page marvel called Effective Parenting has made a definite change in the way I deal with my children ... although the book is a sort of self learning book but not for a single paragraph one gets bored and can leave the book. Points given in the book are very practical and are elaborated with real life examples. I have recommended this book to a number of parents of my students.

Mahesh Kandpal

Former Principal

Sainik School, Tilaiya

I am writing to congratulate you on bringing out a brilliant book on Effective Parenting. You deserve all the accolades of parent community as well as teachers who always suffer due to communication gap between them and the children. It is a lighthouse for all those concerned with the education of children.

H.L. Chopra

Former Principal

Hyderabad Public School, Hyderabad (A.P.)

My kudos to you for bringing out an excellent book for the guidance of parents. If every parent acts on the advice given in this book no child can go astray_they will all become masterpieces.

Satish Goyal

Parent

Lotus Valley International School, Noida

An extraordinary collection of the most essential, effective and practical guidelines to bring up your child!

The book is an intensive study of children's all round development and covers almost every nuance of the tightrope journey each parent has to take in raising happy and healthy children in today's world.

Being a mother of two happy grown up children and an educator, I would say, this book is a Bible to every present and future parent. If parents follow Mr. Arora's advice in letter and spirit, their children will grow up as inquisitive and discerning individuals.

Manju Thareja

Sector 40, Noida

I have known Mrs. & Mr. Arora for over 20 years. They have brought up their two children in an exemplary manner: both of them doing exceedingly well in life.

This is what Mr. Arora has written in his book "Effective Parenting". The book not only effectively brings out the situations parents face while rearing them, but also offers solutions on how to tackle them. I have myself brought up my two children as per the advice Mr. Arora enunciates in this easy to read book. I have been delighted with their progress. The children of those parents who care to read "the book" will find firm ground on which to stand _ the ground of their own identities and integrity, of their soul. They will have been fortified with values and life skills. With this type of upbringing they will be able to face courageously the vicissitudes of life.

Ruchi Sibbal

Palm Grove Apartments

Sector 50, Noida